wise concoctions

Natural Elixirs and Tonics for Health and Energy

BY BONNIE TRUST DAHAN

Photographs by Rita Maas

CHRONICLE BOOKS

SAN FRANCISCO

Library of Congress
Cataloging-in-Publication Data:

Dahan, Bonnie.

Wise concoctions: natural elixirs
and tonics for health and energy/
by Bonnie Dahan;
photographs by Rita Maas.

120 p.   17.8 x 20.3 cm.

Includes bibliographical
references and index.

ISBN 0-8118-1744-X

1. Beverages—Therapeutic use.
2. Tonics (Medicinal preparations).
I. Title.

RM239.D34 1999
615'.321—dc21
98-11973
CIP

Printed in Hong Kong

Designed by Laurie Frankel
Food styling by William L. Smith
Prop styling by Barbara Fritz

Distributed in Canada by
Raincoast Books
8680 Cambie Street
Vancouver, British Columbia V6P 6M9

10 9 8 7 6 5 4 3 2 1

Chronicle Books
85 Second Street
San Francisco, California 94105

www.chroniclebooks.com

DEDICATION

To Yael and Omri, my wisest of all concoctions.

ACKNOWLEDGMENTS

Those who contributed to and inspired *Wise Concoctions* extend beyond this list to cultures far and wide and back in time to many bygone eras. As for contemporary cohorts who helped make this book possible, certainly my most generous benefactor of innumerable hours of his time and unflagging, good-natured support is Stephen Yafa, wordsmith, patient editor, and loving husband. Is there a male counterpart to the Muse? Omri Dahan, son and chief researcher, explored the dusty stacks of university archives for obscure volumes that generated rich information and anecdotes for the historical text. Yael Dahan, daughter-away-at-college, offered her unwavering loyalty, tasting, and photography services. Genevieve Morgan, friend and author, provided encouragement for the initial idea and additional valuable research. My gratitude also goes to nutritionist Kate Plager, who brainstormed with me at the outset, suggested ingredients, and tested numerous recipes that became part of the final selection. Ed Bauman, head of the Institute for Educational Therapy, checked the recipes thoroughly for accuracy and efficacy and donated three of his own. Nam Singh, Chinese herbal cooking expert and my teacher, offered original and traditional recipes from his extraordinary repertoire. Other herbalists and dear friends unselfishly shared their favorite concoctions and treasured family secrets. While I may have taken "culinary license" with them, please know that it was with the best of intentions to make them more accessible for a wider audience. I also thank Charlotte Sheedy, dear friend and literary agent, who always understood the value in this collection and shepherded it to its eventual home at Chronicle Books. Finally, my greatest appreciation goes to family members and friends for their discerning taste buds and forbearance during the last two years.

Rose Hips Lemonade, page 72

Contents

Preface

My personal introduction to the healing power of infused herbs began twenty-five years ago, during a trip to Morocco, when I became violently ill with stomach cramps and remorseful that I had ignored warnings to bring along that era's prescription drug of choice for dysentery. I looked skeptically at the steaming glass of freshly brewed *zatar* tea that my future mother-in-law urged on me. Born in a tiny, remote village at the edge of the Sahara Desert, she had raised nine children without the benefit of trained doctors or organized medical care. Despite the primitive conditions, they had all grown to be healthy adults, thanks, in part, to their mother's inherited knowledge of a half-dozen accessible herbs—or so I was told. Faced with no sensible alternatives, I drank her potion quickly and waited for the results. To my surprise, within an hour, my cramps subsided and I was able to get out of bed.

Two years later I was pregnant with my first child and determined, like other mothers of my generation, to deliver my baby through drug-free natural childbirth. By questioning màny seemingly sacrosanct practices and symptom-related medications that did not necessarily take into account the needs of the whole person, I became versed in a few natural solutions that offered choices less intrusive than traditional medicine. But, had I known then what I've since learned, I also would have been drinking raspberry leaf tea as a uterine tonic during the latter part of my pregnancy, and added in some borage leaf, fennel, and alfalfa to facilitate lactation. By the late 1970s, as a practicing vegetarian, I began to seek out and acquire an in-depth knowledge of good nutrition and information about the healthful benefits of individual herbs.

As the years passed, and the needs of my growing family changed, my assortment of remedies and preventative practices grew more substantial. Now, twenty-five years after I experienced my first herbal brew in Morocco, when I or any member of my family is coming down with a cold, I automatically reach for the echinacea and Pickled Garlic Elixir (page 22). After dinner in the summer, I pick fresh, organic lemon verbena from my garden and infuse it as a calming digestive. I sip an orange blossom tisane that I hand-carried back from Paris because the herbalist at the Palais Royal assured me it would bring restful nights and sweet dreams. It does.

Like countless others, I seek a healthier lifestyle supported by an accumulation of information aimed at promoting vitality and longevity. Over the years, after collecting hundreds of recipes, I have come to think of them as "Wise Concoctions" mostly because they work, but also because they originate from the hands-on, centuries-old collective wisdom of a variety of indigenous cultures. The ancient Mayans drank frothing bowls of chocolate laced with pepper for fortitude; Taoist priests attributed their longevity in part to the use of Chinese wolfberries in cooking and teas; and no matter what your heritage, everyone's grandmother swears by her own cure-all recipe for soup. The recent proliferation of juice bars is a more current example of our impulse to soothe our ills and strengthen our bodies in a palatable liquid form.

To make this compendium complete and beneficial for a wide range of personal health concerns, I sought out the help of several expert herbalists and nutritionists. While the recipes you find here are not panaceas or substitutes for professional medical care, they are intended to make the possibilities of prevention and vibrant health as accessible as your kitchen pantry.

Finally, I have noticed there is also some ineffable benefit that comes from the manner in which you prepare these concoctions. The simple act of creating a healthful beverage or broth to remedy a current ailment or forestall a future one is in itself life enriching. By selecting the very best ingredients—fresh, organic vegetables and fruits, the highest quality herbs, purified or spring water—and presenting them in your most esthetically pleasing crockery or crystal, you are already contributing to the practices of good health and well-being. Perhaps the most important ingredient of all is the measure of good intention and love that each of these recipes invites.

Herbal remedies and folk cures have always been rooted in a communal instinct, and it is in this same spirit that I offer them. While many of these recipes date back several hundred years, I hope you find them as relevant to your life today as they were when their powers to heal were first discovered. The drinks and broths that I've selected address daily needs and focus on healing through nourishment to promote health, vitality, and balance. In the end, this is a book about wellness from the inside out.

Introduction

Before the world invented high-tech diagnostic instruments and a dietary supplement industry, and long before we had to go to an alternative market to find "natural" food, human beings by instinct took care of their own health and well-being by stepping outdoors. Foraging, harvesting, and creating remedies from plants close to home, they began an oral tradition of kitchen medicinals that has been passed down from one generation to the next. Eventually, these cures and preventatives were formalized into "herbals" that became treasured family heirlooms.

The elixirs and tonics that follow honor this ancient healing legacy and adapt it to suit our contemporary lifestyle. From the thousands of possible selections, those you'll find here can be quickly assembled and easily prepared. My intention is to invite you to take an informed look at many beneficial herbs, spices, and foods that you might already have in your pantry and to introduce you to others with tonifying and healing properties that you may not know about. Culled from around the world, these recipes utilize an array of fruits, vegetables, and herbs to promote good health through plant chemistry, which fortifies and heals our bodies, stimulates energy, and brings clarity to our thought processes. Some strengthen the immune system while others help correct imbalance or ease the symptoms of various ailments. The information that is supplied in these pages should help you to choose the most efficient drink or broth for a particular purpose. In addition, all that is needed is an adventurous spirit and an enthusiasm for taking control of your day-to-day personal well-being. Each recipe includes concise directions for its intended use as well as an explanation of how the ingredients work. Although versions of some of these recipes have been in use for at least five thousand years in one form or another according to recorded history, when I began to collect them, I discovered that there were no precise definitions for "tonics" and "elixirs." In fact, the terms were often used interchangeably, especially in the marketplace. A wine-based Chinese "elixir" to ease gastric distress, for example, would be called a digestive "tonic" in France. To keep things simple, for the purposes of this book, I have established my own definitions, based on history and folk tradition, to distinguish between the two terms.

You'll find that the recipes in this book are categorized by their effect on the body and mind as follows:

ELIXIRS	TONICS
are healing remedies; they address situations of imbalance and symptoms of illness.	promote overall good health and balance; they fortify your system and keep you feeling fit and well.

There is a very good reason that liquids have been employed as a vehicle for healing. They provide the speediest delivery system to the bloodstream. Also, because they go down easily, fluids like Almond Elixir (page 24) have been used in folk medicine for centuries to provide nourishment to the feverishly ill who cannot tolerate solid foods. Broths and warm beverages comfort us when all looks bleak, warming our bodies as they soothe our souls. Cooling beverages, on the other hand, invigorate us, supplying needed replenishment or offering relaxation and refreshment.

The heft of the cup or bowl, the smoothness imparted to our fingers cupped around it, the tactile security of a familiar object for the hands to hold as the mind roams all contribute to the other creature comforts that wise concoctions offer through taste and touch. How many of us have moved our faces toward the steam of a hot cup of tea and inhaled its rich fragrance or pressed a frosty glass of lemonade to a perspiring cheek? Juices, infusions, smoothies, brews, teas, broths, liqueurs—it hardly matters what form the liquid takes. These elixirs and tonics are also wise because they bolster our strengths and repair our ailments. We drink or sip them, hot or cold, late at night or shortly after waking, for any of a hundred reasons. Through them we experience and enjoy an intimacy between our senses and the natural world that has provided us with its bounty. And we feel better, as we should, for they allow us to pause for a moment to minister to our own individual needs and in doing so to pay gentle and respectful attention to ourselves.

Elixirs

Elixirs have long captured our imaginations. For some, they evoke images of bottled waters from European spas set in romantic mountain locales, where natural healing springs bubble from the depths of the earth and are reputed to magically restore health. For others, elixirs conjure up medieval alchemists fiddling with beakers of strange, dark "aqua vitae" potions that centuries ago were believed to turn base metals into gold and prolong life. It seems, in fact, that most cultures have created a folklore around potent brews and mysterious liquids, often ascribing their miraculous powers to deities who bestowed them on suffering humans. While the elixirs in this section may not be heaven-sent, they have a well-deserved reputation for easing the symptoms of a variety of mortal ailments, and some even soothe and nurse the weary spirit as well as the rasping throat.

In ancient China, where the elixir tradition was first recorded, tribal shamans, or "medicine men," believed that mountain mists contained potent amounts of *qi*, or vital essence, and that by ingesting herbs grown on mountains, sickly humans might replenish their supply of essential life-energy and recover from spiritual and physical disease. Over time, the written Chinese character for "sorcery" was altered to mean both "wine" and "doctor," symbolizing the belief that alcohol-based herbal formulas remedied a variety of conditions. The doctor-wine association proved to be remarkably accurate: the alcohol that results from fermenting fruits and grains extracts out the essence of herbs, and these herbal concentrations, or elixirs, are quickly absorbed into the bloodstream.

Numerous other civilizations also closely studied nature and developed elaborate systems to benefit from its healing attributes. Vegetable and fruit juices gained prominence in the Indian Ayurvedic medical tradition for their ability to speed recovery from illness. By A.D. 70 in ancient Rome, Pliny the Elder was recommending over fifty herbal concoctions as cures for everything from scorpion stings to mad dog bites. During Europe's Dark Ages, Benedictine monks and other monastic orders distilled liqueurs that were often infused with herbs and drunk as medicines. Starting in the sixteenth century, the Europeans who settled the New World brought with them plant-based curatives that soon became entwined with native remedies in both North and South America.

Wherever elixirs traveled, a rich tradition of improbable and astonishing cures tagged along. Together, they produced one of America's most colorful characters, the snake-oil salesman, whose bright yellow wagon contained panaceas for every malady. Or so he claimed. If any of his alcohol-based patent medicines seemed to take the edge off pain, at least for the short term, it was most likely the alcohol speaking. No longer greatly diluted as a vehicle for herbal extracts, it often became the only active ingredient, and by the early 1900s, elixirs were viewed with suspicion if not outright skepticism by many Americans. Lydia Pinkham didn't help the situation. The immense popularity of her famous Vegetable Compound—to help women "go smiling through" their menstrual cramps—was eventually damaged by a magazine exposé that revealed the elixir to be nearly 40 proof. The irony was that Lydia Pinkham's compound also included useful gynecological herbs like black cohosh root, fenugreek, and false unicorn root, which she obtained from the Algonquin Indians.

Today, elixirs are still with us and more relevant than ever to the way we live. In this section, elixirs are defined as hot or cold beverages and broths that take advantage of nature's organic factories—the plant world—to alleviate the discomfort of various maladies and make us feel better. Elixirs do their good work by muting the symptoms of illness and helping to bring your system back into balance. By any name, and at any proof, elixirs have, of course, long since woven their way into the fabric of most societies. Whether a Jewish grandmother's recipe for chicken soup from a Russian shtetl or Nuria's Soupe à Soigner (page 41), elixirs from every part of the world trace their origins back to the basic human impulse to heal our bodies quickly and to give comfort in the process.

The elixirs that follow, some herbal and some concocted from fruits, roots, vegetables, and assorted natural ingredients, provide a safe and effective alternative to over-the-counter medications. They keep alive the heritage of simple, home-based remedies that really work. This kitchen tradition is one that I fervently believe deserves to be honored and respected. The experience of testing these recipes in my own kitchen and dispensing the results to family and friends was often healing in its own right. I found that as I ground herbs, brewed up batches of roots and twigs, and peeled countless cloves of garlic, my own body and mind became centered, and in that way, the elixirs that I created became a peace offering to my soul as well as a gift of compassion to others in a time of need. My hope is that you will try them and that they will do the same for you.

Cold, Flu, and Allergy Symptoms

Today's pharmacy contains aisles of over-the-counter remedies that attempt to combat the devious rhino virus or cold bug by reducing symptoms that cause misery and discomfort. There is often a price to pay in side effects, however: drowsiness, impaired reasoning powers, and dried-out mucous membranes. The recipes I have included here allow you to stay focused and alert, and to avoid dehydration while easing sniffles, coughs, and fever.

I have varied them to include both complex, powerfully effective herbal remedies whose ingredients may not be readily at hand and simpler concoctions that can be prepared quickly, when you need them, from foodstuffs you're likely to have in your pantry: grapefruits, almonds, and cinnamon, by way of example. Two of my favorites are the Chinese Winter Pear Elixir, which is a treat as well as a treatment, and the cooling Almond Elixir, which replenishes spent energies with protein while relieving a fever. While everyone seems to have a preferred secret cold potion, after exhaustive research and a good amount of experimentation, these are the ones I have come to rely on most.

Apple Tea, page 19

DECOCTION GUIDE

Use a decoction for roots, bark, twigs, and berries that require a longer extraction process than seeds, leaves, and flowers to activate their beneficial properties.

1. Fill a saucepan with one-third more purified water than the final volume you want to make. Bring the water to a rolling boil.

2. Crush the herbs using a mortar and pestle. Do not use a food processor.

3. Add the herbs and boil for about 5 minutes. Reduce the heat and simmer, uncovered, for 15 minutes. Strain and serve hot or cold.

INFUSION GUIDE

While there are several theories on how to make the perfect infusion, most are quite similar. You can experiment to determine what works best for you.

1. Start with the best herbs available. Use about 1 teaspoon dried herbs or 2 teaspoons fresh herbs for each 1 cup purified water. If making more than 1 cup, place the herbs in a glass or earthenware pot. Avoid using metal pots; they can release harmful chemicals into the infusion.

2. Bring the purified water barely to a boil in a saucepan. Remove from the heat (vigorously boiling water can evaporate the herb's active components into the steam), and pour into the pot or cup.

3. Let steep, covered, for at least 5 minutes. Unless specifically noted, you can steep most herbs for as long as you like. The infusion will just get stronger and more flavorful with time. Experience and personal taste will guide you.

4. Strain and serve the infusion. Many are just as good on ice. For iced infusions, double the ratio of herbs to water and serve on ice; or use the ratio above and let chill overnight in the refrigerator.

Allergy Helper

COLD, FLU, AND ALLERGY SYMPTOMS

The combination of herbs used here, rich in minerals and phytochemicals, reduces swelling of the mucous membranes and supports the immune function, which allows your body to better clear toxins. Echinacea prompts the immune system to kick in, while the wild cherry bark acts as a cough suppressant. Bioflavonoids (page 62), found in the white part of citrus rinds, also act as anti-inflammatory agents. Licorice, used to balance the flavors of the other ingredients, helps soften and soothe the mucous membranes and eases the discomfort of sore throats, hoarseness, and wheezing. Using local honey is important in this recipe because it helps you to become desensitized to the pollens in your area.

> **Bring the water to a boil and add the herbs and orange rind. Let boil for approximately 5 minutes and then simmer for 15 minutes. Strain, stir in the honey, and drink hot or cold.**

MAKES 3 CUPS

4 cups purified water

1 teaspoon wild cherry bark

1 teaspoon echinacea root

1 teaspoon licorice root

1 teaspoon white inner part of orange rind

1 teaspoon local honey

Citrus Remedy

If an herbal approach seems too complicated, here is a quick and easy way to receive a very concentrated dose of bioflavonoids (see page 62), which will act as natural anti-inflammatories to reduce the swelling of tissues and ease the severity of allergy symptoms. You will also be fortifying yourself with a good dose of vitamin C if you eat the peeled fruit.

> **Place the minced peels and water in a saucepan. Cover and simmer for 20 minutes. Stir in the honey to taste when slightly cooled. Store in a glass jar with a lid in the refrigerator for up to one week. Use 1 teaspoon three times per day.**

MAKES 3 CUPS

Peels from 3 grapefruits, finely minced (a food processor makes this easy)

Peels from 3 lemons, finely minced

1½ cups purified water

½ to ¾ cup local honey

Apple Tea

Among other proven health benefits, the cooling nature of apples has made them an ideal antidote for fevers. Since the second century B.C., apple infusions have been used to reduce fevers. Children enjoy the sweet flavor of this nutritious tea when they are ill. You don't have to wait for a cold to take pleasure from this simple, delicious brew. One cup (or more) a day may help keep your fever away.

> **Place the apples and cold water in a heatproof jar and cover. Set the jar in a saucepan and pour in the boiling water. Simmer for 2 hours. Remove from the heat and strain. Add the lemon juice and honey and drink hot.**

MAKES 3 CUPS

2 or 3 cooking apples, peels intact, cored and sliced

3 cups cold purified water

2 cups boiling water

1 teaspoon freshly squeezed lemon juice

1 teaspoon honey

Elderflower Spritzer

Wines, syrups, cordials, jams, and medicinal tisanes have been created from the flowers and berries of the elder plant. I remember being spared from an impending case of jet lag one summer after an all-night flight to London by the bracing effect of an iced elderflower lemonade. This version is a perfect antidote to summer colds as the elderflowers encourage sweating and, in combination with yarrow and mint, help relieve upper respiratory congestion. The astringent action of the lemon helps tissues to contract so that mucous is released, which helps cleanse and purify the system. Lemons are also high in vitamin C. Honey, an antiseptic that deters germ growth, soothes and sweetens this elixir.

> Bring the water to a boil and pour over the herbs. Allow to steep for 5 minutes or longer. (For a hot drink, simply add the lemon and honey and eliminate the next step.)

> To make the spritzer, add the lemon and honey, and allow the infusion to cool in the refrigerator. When ready to drink, add the carbonated water and stir. Garnish with the mint sprig.

MAKES 1 1/2 CUPS

1 cup purified water

1 teaspoon dried elderflowers

1/2 teaspoon fresh or dried peppermint leaves

1/2 teaspoon yarrow leaves

Juice from 1/2 lemon

1 teaspoon honey

1/2 cup carbonated mineral water

Sprig of fresh mint

Pickled Garlic Elixir

COLD, FLU, AND ALLERGY SYMPTOMS

MAKES 1½ CUPS

2 heads elephant garlic cloves, separated into cloves and peeled

½ cup honey

½ cup organic apple cider vinegar

1 teaspoon tamari

Garlic is a natural immune system stimulant and antibiotic. This folk remedy comes from the California School of Herbal Studies. The pickling liquid helps soothe cold symptoms; dilute it with hot water and a pinch of cayenne. As a preventative, the garlic cloves can be eaten like pickles, and the liquid mixed in salad dressings. Avoid during pregnancy.

> **Put the garlic in a 1 ½-cup mason jar. Mix the honey, vinegar, and tamari. Pour over the garlic to cover. Close the top securely and refrigerate for six to eight weeks. The elixir can be refrigerated for up to six months.**

Chinese Winter Pear Elixir

MAKES 1 CUP

1 bosc or red Bartlett pear

1 teaspoon rock sugar

1 cup purified water

1 tablespoon rice wine (optional)

A seasonal remedy using pears that are ripe in winter, this old Chinese elixir reduces coughs and excessive phlegm. According to Traditional Chinese Medicine, both pears and sugar are cooling, and as a result, they clear the spleen so it will not produce too much mucous. The rock sugar strengthens the spleen and the rice wine stimulates circulation.

> **Cut the pear in half and core, leaving the stem. Fill the hole in each half with the sugar. Place the pear in a saucepan and add the water and the rice wine, if using. Cover and boil for 15 to 20 minutes. Strain and drink; eat the pear.**

Almond Elixir

MAKES 2 CUPS

¼ cup organic almonds

2 cups plus 3 or 4 tablespoons cold purified water

1 teaspoon honey

Throughout history, across many cultures, almonds appear in a remarkably versatile range of remedial recipes. There is an old Middle Eastern saying that "You can travel any distance without food, as long as your pockets are full of almonds." High in linoleic acid, an essential fatty acid needed for the body's biochemistry, almonds are a good source of calcium and vitamin E. This recipe is also recommended for a cold or upper respiratory infection, especially when accompanied by a fever, because it provides soothing sustenance while cooling body temperature and quenching thirst. Some Ayurvedic recipes, made with milk and spices, include almonds because they are valued for their rejuvenating power. A version of this drink, which combines bitter and sweet almonds, is found at North African celebrations; yet another, combined with milk, is imbibed on sweltering hot summer afternoons to assuage both hunger and thirst.

> Crush the almonds in a food processor or blender until they are quite fine. Add the cold water, 1 tablespoon at a time, until a paste is formed.

> Boil the remaining 2 cups water. Very slowly add the boiling water to the almond paste, stirring continuously. Stir in the honey. Let the mixture cool, then blend until frothy and serve.

Sister Rose's Cajun Cough-Stopper

When my good friend Rita Capponi heard I was collecting recipes for this book, she insisted I try this remedy for a no-fail, sleep-through-the-night toddy. Created by her aunt, Sister Rose, a nun in a New Orleans Dominican convent—whom Rita nominates for sainthood on the basis of this recipe—the prized toddy was a closely guarded family secret until now. The spices recommended by Sister Rose all have warming qualities, which help combat viral distress when combined with the vitamin C in the orange juice. Rita remembers fondly the precision with which the toddy directions were dispensed by Sister Rose whenever anyone was coming down with a cough or cold. Besides the bourbon, it seems that timing is the most important ingredient here. According to Capponi family legend, the instant you feel the first tickle in your throat, you must mix up this powerful elixir, climb into bed with a towel wrapped around your neck to ward off chills, and sip the toddy slowly. Guaranteed to get you through the night.

> **Add the spices to the juice and mix well. Bring the mixture to a boil, pour into a cup, and add the honey. Add the bourbon. Inhale the steam and sip very slowly.**

MAKES 1 CUP

¼ teaspoon ground cinnamon

¼ teaspoon ground nutmeg

¼ teaspoon ground allspice

¾ cup freshly squeezed orange juice (or orange, grapefruit, and lemon juice combined)

1 teaspoon honey

¼ cup bourbon

Sunflower Seed Cough Quieter

MAKES 1 1/2 CUPS

¼ cup sunflower seeds

1-inch piece fresh ginger root

4 cups purified water

1 teaspoon honey

1 tablespoon brandy (optional)

Although the healing properties of sunflowers were not yet known to Europeans when they first arrived from Central America in the sixteenth century, their reputation as a bronchial folk remedy soon began to spread, particularly throughout Russia. Centuries later, scientific research has confirmed that inulin, one of the constituents in sunflowers, works as a treatment for the wheezing often associated with asthma. In this helpful cough elixir, sunflowers are combined with ginger, a warming catalyst that acts as an expectorant for the lungs by breaking up mucus or phlegm. Honey is added as a soothing ingredient and allows the brew to slide more easily down an irritated sore throat, which often accompanies a cough.

> **Combine the sunflower seeds, ginger, and water. Bring to a boil and then simmer until reduced by more than half. Let cool and then strain. Add the honey and stir to mix. At this point, the more adventurous (or desperate) sometimes add the brandy; its medicinal effects are purely anecdotal.**

NOTE: This remedy is in no way meant to treat asthma, a serious medical condition that requires a doctor's care.

Sniffle Chaser Broth

This broth is a delicious vegetarian alternative to chicken soup. It contains four ingredients that provide relief from cold symptoms. Shiitakes contain all eight amino acids as well as B vitamins and are a good source of the trace mineral germanium, which helps the body to resist disease by stimulating immune functions such as white blood cell production. While the Romans dubbed mushrooms "food of the gods," in Chinese medicine shiitakes are used as immune strengtheners that fortify the blood and *chi* (defined as "vital essence" or "life force") to help fight infection. Ginger is known for its warming qualities that invigorate the circulatory system and for its effectiveness in clearing respiratory ailments. Astragalus, a very popular Chinese herb, enhances the immune system and provides revitalizing energy. Garlic has antibiotic properties, and miso, a fermented soybean paste, provides flavor to this delicious and smooth broth and additional immune fortification.

> Soak the mushrooms in 2 cups of the water for 20 minutes. Do not discard the soaking liquid, as it contains the essence of the mushrooms' "medicine." Bring the remaining 6 cups water to a boil and add the ginger, garlic, and astragalus. Reduce the heat to a simmer. Mix the miso with 8 tablespoons of the hot liquid to form a smooth paste. Add the miso, mushrooms, and mushroom soaking liquid to the herbs and water. Simmer for 30 minutes. Strain and drink hot. The broth can be stored in the refrigerator for two days.

MAKES 8 CUPS

6 dried shiitake mushrooms

8 cups purified water

3-inch piece fresh ginger root, sliced thinly

6 cloves garlic

6 pieces shaved astragalus root

4 teaspoons light miso

Headaches and Hangovers

Lavender, that exquisitely scented flowering herb of many talents, is frequently called on for its calming properties as well as its sensory pleasures. I have discovered it to be helpful as a relief from stress headaches in an infusion blended with St. John's wort, skullcap, and lemon verbena. You can rely on the actions of these herbs to dilate the constricted capillaries that cause most common headaches and to soothe the anxiety or tension that often causes the headache in the first place. They accomplish this without producing the slightly unfocused or cottony sensation that some experience from analgesics. Then, too, there is another kind of healing that comes when you put your feet up and enjoy a steaming mug of fragrant herbs, a soul-nurturing comfort that transcends medical science. I've also included hangover remedies that cleanse impurities from the liver while soothing our battered nerves.

Headache Calmer

MAKES 2 CUPS

½ teaspoon dried skullcap leaves

½ teaspoon dried lemon verbena leaves

½ teaspoon dried lavender flowers

½ teaspoon dried St. John's wort leaves

2 cups purified water

1 teaspoon honey

For headaches caused by stress, try this systemic approach that calms as it alleviates pain. Skullcap is an herb that relaxes the central nervous system and generally acts as a sedative. Lavender is soothing and cooling and has long been prescribed to create internal balance. (A few drops of pure lavender essential oil mixed with almond oil gently rubbed on the temples while drinking this brew will speed recovery.) Lemon verbena is a digestive herb that is mildly sedative, and St. John's wort, a proven antidepressant, repairs frazzled nerves.

> **Mix the herbs. Bring the water to a boil. Pour over herbs and steep for 10 minutes. Strain and add the honey. Drink iced or hot.**

Coffee Headache Elixir

White willow bark helps offset a "coffee headache" and calms the jitters. Native Americans have used it for hundreds of years to cure pain, and now we know why: it contains salicin, the major ingredient in aspirin. Sage is an effective natural "nervine" used to calm and strengthen the nervous system, while chamomile adds a relaxing and pleasant aroma. Lemons, high in vitamin C and astringent, are excellent for any kind of "detox."

> **Bring the water to a boil. Add the herbs and steep for 20 minutes. Strain. Add the lemon juice and honey to taste. Drink 1 to 2 cups in the morning and evening. Store in the refrigerator.**

MAKES 4 CUPS

4 cups purified water

1 tablespoon white willow bark

1 teaspoon fresh or dried sage leaves

1 teaspoon chamomile flowers

Juice of ½ lemon

Honey

Chinese Spearmint and Egg Broth

The Chinese have long used spearmint in a tea or broth for its nerve-calming properties and as a remedy for stress headaches. This simple recipe combines the cooling nature of mint with egg protein, which gives the broth its body and makes it a unique and tasty variation of egg drop soup.

> **Bring the water to a boil. Reduce the heat and mix in the egg and spearmint. Simmer and rake the egg with a fork until it is cooked. Strain the broth and sip while hot.**

MAKES 1 CUP

1 cup purified water

1 egg, beaten

2 teaspoons fresh or 1 teaspoon dried spearmint leaves

Morning-After Decoction

Try this brew when you have imbibed beyond your limit and feel dragged down by the low-energy hangover blues. You will find it most effective if sipped all morning long, especially when the thought of solid food turns your stomach. The herbal blend of ingredients used in this elixir supports the liver, which is depleted by alcohol consumption. The liver, considered the master gland of detoxification, filters impurities in the blood. Dandelion root and leaves have been used for centuries to cleanse the liver. Burdock root, a powerful blood purifier, also has nutritive qualities. Licorice root has been used in Chinese medicine for thousands of years as a strengthening herb for the kidneys, but it also helps them to filter toxins released by the liver. It mixes well with the other ingredients to smooth out and sweeten their slightly bitter taste.

> Bring the water to a boil. Pour over the herbs and steep for 30 minutes. Strain. Drink 4 cups over the course of the day.

MAKES 4 CUPS

4 cups purified water

1 to 2 teaspoons chopped dried burdock root

1 to 2 teaspoons chopped fresh or dried dandelion leaves and chopped dried root

1 to 2 teaspoons licorice root

Indigestion and Stomach Cramps

Stomach ills are an international phenomenon, with abundant folk remedies from countries everywhere. This section offers a sampling drawn from several widespread cultures. From North Africa comes zatar, a form of thyme that has proven to be an immediate aid for cramps and diarrhea. Soupe à Soigner is a traditional Catalan recipe based on the digestive properties of garlic, while kudzu, a natural, culinary thickening agent, is the primary ingredient in an Asian remedy for nausea. Also included is a fennel and chamomile recipe that dates back to medieval England. In fact, many of the ingredients in these recipes, like ginger, have been used to ease stomach distress for thousands of years. Although it is reassuring to learn that some of their beneficial effects are now being given scientific sanction in laboratories around the world, kitchen sages throughout history have already taught us that a quick trip to the pantry or herb rack can often do wonders to placate an upset tummy.

Fennel-Chamomile Tisane, page 35

Tisanes

Well-being, in its purest form, has long been the province of scented teas. Boiling water poured over a leaf or flower can transform a plant into a palliative. The word itself, *tisane*, is a historical French name for herbal teas. For centuries horehound, sage, mullein, and marshmallow, among other herbs, have been brewed into tisanes to relieve pulmonary and respiratory complaints. Upset stomachs have been soothed by Greek oregano, caraway, peppermint, marjoram, and half a dozen other herbs as well. Meadowsweet, lavender, and lemon balm have passed down through generations as helpful herbs for headaches. Tisanes were also practical because the herbs they were made from grew wild or were cultivated in kitchen gardens.

Tisanes have not always been concocted from single herbs. Many, in fact, mix and mingle numerous herbs into a brew prepared for a particular purpose: a good night's sleep, for example. It will hardly come as a surprise that we owe our own national legacy of herbal infusion lore to Native Americans, who lived not only on the land, but in harmony with it. Virtually all first-person accounts of Native American medicine from the eighteenth and nineteenth centuries include descriptions of tea preparation—sometimes for ceremonial reasons, but most commonly to soothe and repair. Such herbs as boneset, purple coneflower, and goldenseal have been passed down to us directly from tribal healing traditions, along with black cohosh for relaxing the nervous system. While many tisanes are currently available on the shelves of gourmet and natural food markets as boxed tea bags and in bulk, creating your own blends is a most enjoyable, satisfying experience.

Dill Tisane

While dill adds a distinctive flavor to fish, soups, and salads, its medicinal benefits are concentrated in the seeds, which comprise this straightforward infusion. Often used as a children's colic remedy, the seeds aid digestion and prevent flatulence and hiccups. They also happen to be rich in calcium. Try this subtle tisane after a particularly heavy meal eaten later in the evening because it calms the digestive tract and also helps prevent insomnia.

> **Bring the water to a boil. Pour over the dill seeds and steep for 5 minutes. Strain and drink the tisane. (If you like the taste, you can also eat the seeds.)**

MAKES 1 CUP

1 cup purified water

1 tablespoon dill seeds

Fennel–Chamomile Tisane

If you have ever tried the sugar-coated fennel seeds often served in Indian restaurants at the end of a meal, you know that they act as an effective antidote for indigestion. In fact, fennel seeds have been prized for their ability to aid digestion since the Middle Ages in England, when they were chewed in church to prevent embarrassing gastric sound effects. Here, fennel combines with chamomile, which has a slightly sedative effect on a nervous stomach.

> **Bring the water to a boil and pour over the herbs. Allow to steep for 10 minutes. Strain and drink while warm.**

MAKES 1 CUP

1 cup purified water

½ teaspoon fennel seeds

½ teaspoon dried chamomile flowers

Soft Drinks

The next time you twist open a carbonated soda, you will more than likely be drinking the nutritionally challenged descendant of healing tonics. From root beer to ginger ale, today's soft drinks were yesterday's herbal remedies.

As far back as the eighteenth century, natural spring water—long recognized for its curative properties—was being bottled for sale in both Europe and North America. In the early 1800s, a chemistry professor from Yale perfected his artificial carbonation process and sold his bottled product as a treatment for heartburn and headaches. It was not long before fizzy water was being infused with roots, barks, herbs, berries, and even juices, and peddled as panaceas for everything from hangovers to impotence.

In the absence of federal food-and-drug regulations, extravagant claims could be made with impunity for worthless snake oils; more dangerously, some formulas contained addictive narcotics. One was Coca-Cola, which began life as a carbonated bottled stimulant made from a recipe that included cocaine-laden coca leaf as well as the African kola nut extract. Having created America's national beverage, John S. Pemberton soon learned that he was about to run afoul of new federal laws and quickly produced a nonnarcotic version.

Another favorite stimulant brewed in colonial times, root beer, combined European ingenuity with Native American savvy about healing plants. Sassafras, wintergreen oil, and birch oil were among the first ingredients used. Ginger ale—once sold as a remedy for measles, arthritis, and back conditions—and cream soda also gained initial acceptance as herbal folk medicines; typically these concoctions contained capsicum (which provides the heat in peppers), sarsaparilla, allspice, gentian root, vanilla, and, of course, ginger. There's something comforting to the psyche as well as the stomach about beverages that appear to be whipped up on the back burner of mom's stove, then cooled in a cellar and aged in wood before being carbonated, bottled, and delivered to your grocer's shelf. Perhaps that's why the "home-brewed" folk tradition of sodas is still alive and well in root beers and ginger ales that quench our thirst while they remind us of their humble, natural origins.

Herbal Ginger "Beer"

INDIGESTION AND STOMACH CRAMPS

I remember, as a young child, one of the only benefits of suffering with an upset stomach was the welcome glass of ginger ale offered with a confident promise that it would alleviate my symptoms. While there may not have been enough ginger in that commercial brew to have any effect, there was real medicinal value in the folk wisdom that led to its creation. Ginger has been considered a therapeutic herb for at least two thousand years, and its digestive and antispasmodic properties have led to its reputation as an effective antidote for stomach cramps, indigestion, flatulence, and nausea. Its warming qualities also make it an excellent circulatory and energy stimulant. This recipe, which I learned from herbalist Diana DeLuca, makes a delicious and healthy alternative to store-bought, overly sweetened ginger ales.

> **To make the beer, stir the syrup and lemon juice into the carbonated water until thoroughly mixed. Garnish with the lemon peel.**

MAKES 1 CUP

2 tablespoons Ginger Syrup (recipe follows)

1 tablespoon fresh squeezed lemon juice

1 cup carbonated mineral water

1 slice of lemon peel

GINGER SYRUP

> **Combine the sliced ginger and water and simmer for 30 minutes. Cool slightly, then strain. Add the maple syrup and stir to mix. When completely cooled, refrigerate for up to six months.**

MAKES 4 CUPS
GINGER SYRUP

1½ cups peeled and sliced fresh ginger

4 cups purified water

1 cup pure maple syrup

37

Kudzu Elixir

MAKES 1 CUP

1 teaspoon kudzu starch

1 cup purified water

1 teaspoon umeboshi
plum paste

½ teaspoon fresh ginger juice

Variations of this unconventional recipe come from several different cultures. An invasive plant that grows wild throughout the South, kudzu is claimed to be a panacea for a wide range of disorders from upset stomachs to headaches and hangovers, and for all sorts of muscular aches and pains. In Japan it is a remedy for these and other ills, and in Chinese medicine it is sometimes used in conjunction with acupuncture. Kudzu also curbs sugar and alcohol cravings. Many vegetarian cooks use kudzu as a thickener for gravies and sauces, but here it is combined with ginger and the salty, yet sour umeboshi plum paste to soothe stomach cramps and nausea. The kudzu, ginger, and plum paste all arrest contractions of the intestines, ease cramping, and aid digestion. Ginger juice can easily be made either by grating fresh ginger and squeezing out the juice through cheesecloth or by using a garlic press and straining the juice.

> **Dissolve the kudzu in the water and stir thoroughly. Add the plum paste and bring to a slow simmer, stirring continuously so that the mixture does not separate. After it thickens slightly, the kudzu will become transparent. Continue to simmer over very low heat for another minute. Remove from the heat and stir in the ginger juice. Allow to cool slightly and sip.**

Zatar Tisane

MAKES 1 CUP

1 cup purified water

1 teaspoon dried zatar leaves

This book would be incomplete without an entry for the tisane that originally set me on the path to discover the pleasures and value of wise concoctions. *Zatar*, a form of thyme, is still the most immediate and effective cure that I've come across for the stomach pains and diarrhea associated with foreign travel. It's also useful for simple overindulgence in rich foods. Until recently, I have had little luck finding authentic *zatar* in the United States. After considerable investigation, I learned of a source close to home. Queen of Sheba (see Resource Guide, page 116), a Middle Eastern grocery in San Francisco, will mail-order the herb anywhere in the country. Be sure to specify that it will be used for tea as there is also a culinary mixture with the same name. For me, *zatar* has become as much of a staple in my herbal pantry as aspirin is in a conventional medicine chest.

> **Bring the water to a boil. Pour over the *zatar* and allow to steep for at least 5 minutes. Strain and drink while still hot.**

Nuria's Soupe à Soigner

This traditional Catalan recipe was recounted to me in French (thus the name) by a friend, Nuria, who looks ten or more years younger than her actual age of sixty-five. Whether her strong constitution and irrepressible energy result from drinking this broth can't be medically proven, but I know for certain that Nuria can be frequently found dancing in San Francisco nightclubs until 3 A.M. during her yearly visit, and that's all the evidence I need. When I asked her about any natural remedies from her childhood, Nuria remembered that her Spanish grandmother always made this tasty soup for an upset stomach. While reputed to be a general cure-all, it was mostly used to treat digestive ailments. Needless to say, its efficacy is certainly based on the healing properties of garlic—antibiotic and immune stimulating. Garlic has also been proven effective against diarrhea, certain parasites, and intestinal worms. Here's to good old-fashioned grandmothers' tales and to Nuria's continued good health.

> Combine all the ingredients except the salt and bring to a boil. Simmer until the water is almost absorbed and the broth thickens. Add the salt. Enjoy the benefits of this broth by consuming small amounts very slowly.

MAKES 4 CUPS

1 head garlic, separated into cloves and peeled

3 tablespoons extra virgin olive oil

1 slightly stale baguette or other crusty bread, cut into ½-inch pieces or coarsely chopped in a food processor

5 cups purified water

Pinch of salt

Insomnia

At three in the morning, tossing and turning with a mind racing out of control, I am not great company. Just ask my husband, who could sleep through a twister but awakens with a start when I yank the blanket to my side of the bed in a fit of petulance. If I'm suffering, why shouldn't he? "Be nicer, make lycii," he sometimes mutters in marital shorthand, before dozing off again. He's suggesting I stumble down to the kitchen and make my favorite home brew for insomnia, a milk-based decoction that includes the sweet-tasting Chinese lycii berry and dried red dates. Most nights when insomnia hits, I take his advice. If milk isn't your cup of tea, two other recipes here combat insomnia, one with salad greens and the other with herbs.

Sweet Dreams Elixir

Try these additions to the usual cup of warmed milk the next time you have trouble getting to sleep. In Ayurvedic medicine, milk is considered a nourishing and building food, while its calcium and triptophan content calm and relax. Adding ginger or cinnamon followed by a teaspoon of honey counteracts the mucous that can form if one uses cow's milk. Besides its calming properties, this milk decoction strengthens the digestive system and is extremely nutritive. Lycii, a sweet-tasting Chinese herb available in most Chinatowns or by mail order, is a kidney and liver tonic, high in vitamins A and C, carotene, and linoleic acid. Dried red dates, another Chinese herb, are sweet and warming; they soothe the emotions when you are irritable and help you to drift peacefully into sweet dreams.

> **Heat the milk. Remove seeds from the dates and grind the dates and the lycii with a mortar and pestle or in a blender or food processor. Combine this mixture with the ginger or cinnamon. Add the ground herbs to the heated milk and simmer gently for 15 minutes. Add honey to taste. Strain and sip slowly.**

NOTE: For the Wide-Awake-at-3-a.m. version of insomnia, you may not want to take the time to grind the herbs. I have found a simpler version of this elixir just as effective at those times. Simply simmer the whole herbs in milk for 10 minutes, strain, and stumble back to bed, cup in hand. (The herbs can be eaten; just be careful of the pits in the dates.)

MAKES 1 CUP

1 cup milk, soy milk, or rice milk

3 dried red dates, soaked in warm water to soften

4 lycii berries

1 teaspoon peeled and grated fresh ginger root or ½ teaspoon ground cinnamon

Honey

Green Dreams Tea

Since the time of the ancient Greeks and Romans, lettuce has been regarded as a soporific because of its tranquilizing effects on the nervous system. In fact, this tea is used in the British Isles to combat sleeplessness. If you use the darker, leafier varieties of lettuce, in addition to creating a natural sleep remedy you will be getting the added healthy side effects of chlorophyll, vitamin A, and folic acid as well as calcium, potassium, and iron. The mint aids indigestion, which often leads to insomnia, and also enhances the otherwise bland taste.

> **Bring the water to a boil. Combine the lettuce and mint. Pour the boiling water over the lettuce and mint and steep for 5 minutes. Strain, add honey, and drink while still hot.**

MAKES 1 CUP

1 cup purified water

½ cup finely chopped dark lettuce leaves

2 sprigs of fresh peppermint

Honey

Passionflower-Chamomile Tisane

Most of us have heard about or experienced the calming effects of chamomile for anxiety or stress. When combined with passion-flower, it becomes especially effective. Passionflower, despite its misnomer, actually acts as a sedative for the nervous system. Sip this lovely tisane as a gentle way to ease yourself into a restful night's sleep. Unlike synthetic tranquilizers, it has no lingering effects and is not addictive.

> **Bring the water to a boil. Pour over the herbs. Allow to steep for 10 minutes. Strain and drink while still hot.**

MAKES 1 CUP

1 cup purified water

½ teaspoon dried chamomile flowers

½ teaspoon dried passionflower

Stress and Fatigue

Stress, I have learned, is not simply a state of mind: it can also be a biochemical condition. When our endocrine system senses an external threat, it produces an array of hormones meant to defend us against danger—adrenaline is the best-known example. But these same natural protectors can create problems if they reside in our bloodstream for a prolonged period at high levels. Even if you've managed to keep stress at a distance, it's almost impossible to be fully engaged in today's world without experiencing occasional tension and anxiety, and the depleted feeling that follows it. These recipes help promote equanimity and invigorate frayed nerve endings. By doing so, they can help reduce potentially harmful endocrine levels in our systems. I've included a wide variety of herbs and plants, from kava kava to linden flowers, and even oats, a confirmed comfort food and a friend when the blues get you down.

Lavender and Vervain Tisane

MAKES 1 CUP

1 cup purified water

½ teaspoon dried lavender flowers

½ teaspoon vervain leaves

This tisane combines my two favorite herbs, which together create a balancing effect. The delicate taste of vervain complements the heady evocative quality of lavender to produce a wonderful blend of opposites that attract. Both share the common attributes of easing tension and soothing nerves, which makes this a perfect after-dinner, before-bedtime calmer. If vervain is unavailable, you can substitute lemon verbena for the same effects. Be sure to indulge yourself in the fragrant aroma wafting from the steam, as you relax and imagine the sun setting over the lavender fields of Provence.

> **Bring the water to a boil. Pour over the herbs and allow to steep for 5 minutes. Strain and drink while still hot.**

Hildegard von Bingen

Perhaps the first Western practitioner of what we know today as "holistic medicine," Hildegard von Bingen has recently been rediscovered and popularized for her gifts as a composer of hauntingly eloquent liturgical music. Born in the depths of the Dark Ages, Hildegard emerged as a beacon of wisdom, mysticism, and protean talent. Besides making her mark as a noted poet, musician, composer, author, counselor, mystic, and scholar, she was also an accomplished healer and herbalist.

In 1136, at the age of thirty-eight, von Bingen became the abbess of the Disenbodenberg Benedictine convent. In 1150 she moved the convent to Rupertsberg, near Bingen, the town from which she took her name. Inspired by visions later believed to be caused by severe migraine headaches, Hildegard published numerous poems, interpretations, and music. She also wrote two treatises on medicine and a natural history in which she cataloged over forty-five diseases, along with causes, symptoms, and their treatments. These treatments encompassed more than three hundred plant substances and are thought to be based on medieval herbals and even older texts by Galen, Pliny, and others, as well as local folk and medicinal lore and her own herbal discoveries. She also cultivated a medicinal herbal garden at Rupertsberg.

Hildegard combined her vast working knowledge of herbs and plants with spiritual beliefs, magical incantations, and religious rituals. She often prescribed small doses, "simples," and herbal beverages.

One von Bingen recipe reads, "Whoever cooks lavender with wine . . . or with honey and water, and drinks it lukewarm, it will alleviate the pain in the liver and in the lungs and the steam in the chest. Lavender wine will provide the person with pure knowledge and a clear understanding."

At a time when the average life expectancy was well under forty, Hildegard von Bingen lived into her eighties. She filled those years with extraordinary accomplishment, and forged the foundations for vast areas of medicinal, spiritual, and artistic exploration.

Stress Less Tea

Kava kava is an herb that has gained popularity in recent years due to its ability to relax the central nervous system; it now can be found in most natural food stores. Native to the South Pacific, kava kava tested favorably in European clinical trials for its mood-enhancing effects and has been approved for use there to treat anxiety and insomnia. Peppermint flavors this tea and calms the digestive system.

> **Bring the water to a boil and pour over herbs. Steep for 15 minutes. Strain, add honey, and drink while still hot.**

MAKES 1 CUP

1 cup purified water

½ teaspoon kava kava root

½ teaspoon dried peppermint leaves

Honey, to taste

Basil and Lemon Balm Tisane

These two pungent herbs could just as easily mate as a delicious culinary duo in a vinaigrette dressing. Here they work their botanical magic to reduce tension. Both have antidepressant properties and promote digestion, another comfort to those who tend to have an upset stomach when under stress. Lemon balm is also relaxing and fortifies the nervous system, while basil lifts the spirits and acts as a stimulating tonic.

> **Bring the water to a boil. Pour over herbs and allow to steep for 5 minutes. Strain and serve while still hot.**

MAKES 1 CUP

1 cup purified water

½ teaspoon fresh lemon balm leaves

½ teaspoon fresh basil leaves

Proust's Tilleul

Linden blossoms are known for their ability to calm nervous tension and are frequently brewed alone as a calming tisane known in French as *tilleul*. In fact, Marcel Proust's famed moment of nostalgia that began *Remembrance of Things Past* happened as he dipped a madeleine into a steaming cup of *tilleul*. In this recipe, the linden flowers are mated with other soothing herbs to create a lovely, calming tisane.

> **Bring the water to a boil. Pour over the herbs and allow to steep for 5 to 10 minutes. Strain and drink while hot.**

MAKES 1 CUP

1 cup purified water

½ teaspoon dried linden flowers

½ teaspoon dried lemon balm leaves

½ teaspoon dried chamomile flowers

Celery Antistress Cooler

In the heat of the summer when you're feeling frazzled, this cool drink will help you unwind. The nutrient components of celery regulate, fortify, and calm the nervous system. Carrots also act as a curative for jangled nerves and contribute vitamin A, which boosts the immune system. Vitamin- and mineral-rich apples also contain pectin, which cleanses the system of toxins.

> **Juice all the ingredients. Stir to mix thoroughly. Serve over ice with half a celery or carrot stick as a stirrer.**

MAKES 2 CUPS

10 celery stalks

3 small apples, seeded

2 carrots

Rosemary Spirit Lifter

MAKES 1 CUP

1 cup purified water

2 teaspoons fresh or 1 teaspoon dried rosemary

Freshly squeezed lemon juice

Honey

Rosemary has been valued as a tonic for the brain and circulatory and nervous systems since Greek and Roman days. On mornings when I'm feeling sluggish, I often carry a small vial of rosemary essential oil and inhale a sniff or two for a quick sensory lift. This tisane also comforts the chill associated with an impending cold and soothes a headache.

> **Bring the water to a boil. Pour over the rosemary and steep for 5 minutes. Strain and add lemon juice and sweeten with honey. Drink while hot.**

Shuly's Revitalizing Drink

MAKES 1 1/2 CUPS

1 cup chopped fresh pineapple or canned pineapple chunks in juice

1/2 cup pineapple juice

1-inch piece fresh ginger root, peeled and grated

1 tablespoon freshly squeezed lemon juice

Honey

Shuly, an Israeli friend whose mother is an expert herbalist, passed on this recipe for a refreshing elixir, which originated in Senegal, West Africa. He whips up some of this thick, frothy drink any time he or his friends are feeling low. It is especially energizing (and simply delicious) when you have a virus or are suffering from exhaustion. In addition to pepping you up, the ginger is warming. The lemon is loaded with vitamin C, and the pineapple contains digestive enzymes.

> **Blend all ingredients, including honey to taste, in a blender. Add more juice if you prefer a thinner drink.**

"The Blues" Tisane

With all of the recent health news about oats, it turns out that the spirit as well as the body benefits from eating a steaming bowl of oatmeal. In addition to their confirmed value as comfort food and as an agent that reduces cholesterol, oats have antidepressant properties and are a tonic for the nerves. That recommends them as a valuable antidote to depression and, in tandem with their nutritive attributes, as a wonderful restorative after illness. This unusual tisane combines oatstraw with the tangy taste of vervain, also known to fortify the nervous system and combat depression. Oatstraw, made from the whole plant, which has been dried and chopped, is usually available in the herb section of natural food stores or by mail order. Rolled oats are an acceptable substitute.

> **If using oatstraw, combine the herbs. Bring the water to a boil. Pour over the herbs and allow to steep for up to 10 minutes. If using rolled oats, allow to steep for 20 minutes. Strain, add honey to taste, and drink while still hot.**

MAKES 1 CUP

½ teaspoon dried oatstraw or ¼ cup rolled oats

½ teaspoon dried vervain leaves

1 cup purified water

Honey

Veggie Vitality Cocktail

MAKES 1 CUP

3 to 4 kale leaves

2 tablespoons chopped
fresh parsley

4 carrots, scrubbed but not
peeled

1 apple, seeded but not peeled

One of the reasons juicing has become so popular recently is that it concentrates the vitamins and minerals found in fruits and vegetables so that immediately after drinking them you often can experience a beneficial boost to your system. This particular combination provides magnesium, potassium, and calcium—all rich nutrients that nourish the body. Chlorophyll, which is also plentiful in green leafy vegetables, has a rejuvenating effect. Nourishing to the intestines, it helps filter toxins from the liver. Carrots are rich in vitamin A, which supports the immune system and promotes skin health. The apple adds a sweet taste and contains pectin, another cleansing and purifying agent. You will almost feel the renewed energy coursing through your body as you sip this "cocktail."

> **Put the kale, parsley, carrots, and apple through a juicer. Stir well until the cocktail has a uniform consistency.**

Women's Concoctions

Menstrual cramps can ruin an otherwise perfectly good day. I've included here two recipes for women that offer taste delights in addition to therapeutic aid. You need not stray too far from the produce section, for certain fruits and vegetables—particularly berries and greens—help by boosting levels of magnesium and other important minerals to relieve cramping and offset bladder problems. One juice mixture minimizes the muscular contractions of the uterus and eases menstrual pain, and another alleviates the nausea associated with early pregnancy. Flax seeds, found in the Women's Wisdom Smoothie, contain essential fatty acids that are an asset to women's overall health, and particularly to the smooth functioning of the female reproductive system.

Anticramp Juice Blend

MAKES 1 CUP

2 to 4 collard greens

1 to 2 dandelion leaves

1 tablespoon chopped fresh parsley

2 carrots

The vegetables in this drink offer the necessary magnesium and other minerals that have an antispasmodic effect on the uterus. To boost your magnesium levels when experiencing cramps, try this unusual blend, relax, and sip slowly.

> **Juice all the vegetables and stir to mix thoroughly. Serve immediately.**

Morning Sickness Elixir

Besides the usual advice to nibble on some soda crackers when waking in the morning, here is a remedy that helps with the nausea of morning sickness. This unpleasant side effect has been ascribed to a temporary buildup of toxins, flushed by the liver but not yet eliminated after a night's sleep. Still in the system, they cause discomfort, and so this remedy speeds their elimination. Brewer's yeast, a rich source of easily absorbed vitamin B6 (pyridoxine) as well as other B vitamins, helps liver metabolism. The amount of yeast can be increased according to taste. Tomato juice contains potassium, vitamin C, and vitamin A, as well as some vitamin E, folic acid, and B vitamins, all nourishing nutrients.

> Stir the brewer's yeast into the tomato juice until well blended. Add the lemon juice. Sip slowly.

MAKES 1 CUP

1 teaspoon brewer's yeast

1 cup tomato juice

1 teaspoon freshly squeezed lemon juice or to taste

Phases of the Moon Smoothie

Menstrual cramps can be aided by magnesium, which helps to relax the uterine muscles. Magnesium is most effective when balanced with calcium and potassium. The ingredients in this soothing smoothie are loaded with magnesium, potassium, and iron. Silken tofu, which blends everything into a creamy mixture, also adds protein without too much fat. And the brewer's yeast provides additional nutrients.

> **Blend the banana, berries, tofu, and yeast in a blender until smooth. Add an ice cube while blending if a chilled drink is preferred. Thin with water, if desired.**

MAKES 2 CUPS

1 banana

1 to 2 cups blackberries

3 to 4 ounces silken tofu

1 tablespoon brewer's yeast

Purified water

Women's Wisdom Smoothie

The tofu in this healing smoothie contains healthy amounts of isoflavones, which help to regulate estrogen levels. Flax seeds are rich in essential fatty acids and offer relief from a variety of menopausal symptoms. Their nutrients are best absorbed when ground. Strawberries contribute sweetness and flavor and the added benefits of vitamin C.

> **Blend the strawberries and tofu in a blender until creamy. Blend in the flax seeds. If the smoothie is too thick for your taste, slowly pour in a small amount of purified water until it has the consistency that you prefer.**

MAKES 1 CUP

1 to 2 cups organic strawberries or other berries

4 to 6 ounces silken tofu

1 tablespoon flax seeds, ground

Purified water as needed

Tonics

The essential wisdom of tonics is as down-to-earth as the roots, herbs, seeds, vegetables, fruits, and berries used in their preparation. Preventative medicine is still the best cure. Tonics help keep us in a state of health by strengthening the immune system, stimulating circulation, restoring energy, aiding disgestion, nourishing the blood, and counteracting the negative effects of mental or physical strain, inadequate diet and rest, and environmental toxins.

When our organs and tissues receive a regular and generous supply of the fluids and nutrients they need, they are better equipped to resist attack from intrusive predators—harmful viruses and bacteria. That's what Chinese traditional medical practitioners mean when they talk about maintaining harmony and balance. I think they're worth listening to, because their entire approach to good health depends on warding off diseases before they occur. Like a toned muscle that can withstand sudden impact and respond to an unanticipated challenge, a well-balanced or toned internal system quickly regains its equilibrium when stressed. Herbal tonics are a fundamental part of that four-thousand-year-old strategy.

But, the Chinese are not alone in this belief. As I gathered fortifying and energizing tonic recipes to include here, I soon realized that many other cultures take pride in having developed an elaborate assortment of beverages and liquid foods intended to prevent illness and infection. Indian Ayurvedic medical practitioners have long encouraged muddled patients to drink an infusion of gotu kola (page 112), an herb praised for its brain-sharpening properties. In Medieval England nettles soup was consumed to "spring clean" the body of accumulated winter toxins, a practice still recommended by herbalists today. In the southern regions of the United States, chicory root is brewed to prevent stomach acidity. Everywhere I turned, informed friends and colleagues pointed to new sources of tonic recipes. Of all the recipes suggested to me, the ones that worked (and tasted!) best when I tested them are included here. Some of their ingredients can be found on your spice rack or in your refrigerator produce drawer, and others are easily available in natural food stores and Asian markets or by mail order (see Resource Guide, page 116).

There are a few more points worth knowing about the benefits of tonics. Many do their best work gradually, over a period of months, but the improved sense of well-being and ongoing freedom from illness is well worth the wait. Because they make slow improvements, you may not notice any dramatic effects at first; instead, pay attention to any subtle signs of improved health like more available energy, a feeling of agility and lightness, less moodiness and mental inertia, and, most important, less frequent bouts of colds and flu.

Tonics spring from the earth and, when incorporated into your daily activities, are a constant reminder that the closer we remain in contact with our natural surroundings, the more likely we are to benefit from their resources in order to create our own vitality and well-being. Of course, thousands have gone before me and some have eloquently expressed the importance of respecting all that is available to us to stay healthy. "How much more natural it is to look to the field and the forest for plants and roots to cure our complaints, than to dig in the bowels of the earth and procure certain metals, which prove poisonous and destructive even in obtaining them, and much more so after having been subjected to chemical process," wrote Dr. W. Beach more than 150 years ago in a book for American physicians.

For me, that connection to an age-old tradition of natural wellness resonates well today. There is also something utterly appealing in the idea that by serving ourselves up a life-enhancing potion, we are better equipped to face the stress caused by environmental factors, a lifestyle often dominated by overwork and economic pressures, and the threats of potential illness. Armed with a bunch of parsley, a beet, and a carrot or two, we can easily choose to fortify a depleted system, or with some ginger and pineapple replenish our flagging energy stores. It is reassuring to know that I am not entirely dependent on synthetic compounds that find their way to my bathroom shelf in capsule form sealed in a plastic bottle. Instead, like Dr. Beach, I prefer to look for the vital components of a healthy life in the garden, the farmers' market, and the kitchen.

Resistance

Most of us learn from an early age that our bodies are more likely to resist disease if we eat the right foods and get plenty of exercise and sleep. Terms like bioflavonoids, antioxidants, and phytochemicals may seem to overly complicate that simple, sensible formula, but since each describes an important part of the process, I think they're worth a closer look. I refer to them several times in this chapter.

Found most commonly in the edible pulp of citrus fruits, bioflavonoids strengthen the walls of our capillaries, which link arteries to veins, and allow nutrients to pass through them more easily. One result is that they enhance the absorption of vitamin C into our systems. Antioxidants such as vitamins C and E provide essential nutrients that counteract the damage done by free radicals, unstable molecules that cause cells and tissues to degenerate and make us more susceptible to disease. Phytochemicals, or nutrients delivered by plant food, offer a variety of benefits. Some, like those found in broccoli and other members of the cruciferous family, have proven conclusively to be anticarcinogenic; others help regulate our hormonal activity. Whenever possible, I recommend using organic fruits and vegetables, as they enable you to add phytochemicals to your diet while avoiding potentially harmful synthetic chemicals often found in pesticides.

While resistance to disease takes many forms, this chapter focuses on recipes that fortify our immune systems to help us preserve a state of vibrant health.

Blackberry Hot-Weather Defense, page 64

Blackberry Hot-Weather Defense

MAKES 6 CUPS

6 cups purified water

1 cup fresh blackberries

1 cup dried blackberry leaves

Freshly squeezed lemon juice

6 sprigs of fresh mint

In the mid-to-late summer when blackberries are abundant, consider this unconventional way to use them in addition to making pies and jams. Blackberries, rich with iron, calcium, and magnesium, also contain vitamins A and C, all immune system nutrients. Adding lemon juice to the tea boosts the vitamin C quotient and adds a tartness that balances the sweetness of the blackberries. This simple tea can be served iced or hot.

> **Bring the water to a boil. Add the blackberries and boil for 1 minute. Remove from the heat, add the blackberry leaves, cover, and allow to steep for 5 minutes. Strain and add lemon juice to taste and the mint. Enjoy hot or over ice.**

Chai Resistance Tonic

RESISTANCE

A traditional Indian drink usually made with black tea and aromatic spices, *chai* has become increasingly popular in the West. In this version, which I learned about at the California School of Herbal Studies, the addition of astragalus to the other ingredients enhances its tonic properties. Astragalus, a Chinese herb known as an immune strengthener, increases the production of white blood cells, which defend the body against microorganisms that cause illness. The other spices in *chai* warm and invigorate so that this fragrant mixture stimulates circulation and increases resistance to disease.

> **Bring the water to a boil. Add spice blend. Add as much soy milk as desired and simmer, covered, for 20 minutes. Strain and add the honey.**

CHAI SPICE BLEND

> **Combine all the ingredients and store in a tea tin or airtight jar for up to one year.**

MAKES 1 CUP

1 cup purified water

1 teaspoon Chai Spice Blend (recipe follows)

Soy milk

1 teaspoon honey

MAKES 4 TABLESPOONS SPICE BLEND

2 teaspoons ground cinnamon

2 teaspoons ground cardamom

2 teaspoons dried ginger root

2 teaspoons dried orange peel

2 teaspoons dried astragalus root, broken into small pieces

1 teaspoon whole black peppercorns

1 teaspoon whole cloves

Children's and Seniors' Tonic Tea

MAKES 4 CUPS

4 cups purified water

1 teaspoon dried gingko biloba leaves

1 teaspoon fresh rosemary leaves

1 teaspoon dried St. John's wort leaves

½ teaspoon dried gotu kola leaves

½ teaspoon Siberian ginseng root

Honey

Freshly squeezed lemon juice

Ed Bauman, head of the Institute for Educational Therapy, a training program for nutritionists, created this pleasant blend that increases oxygen to the brain and extremities, improves memory, protects against toxic drugs and chemicals, and brightens the eyes, skin, and hair. He suggests that it can be taken on a regular basis for added alertness and joie de vivre. While this tea is specifically recommended for the more delicate constitutions of children and seniors, its benefits can be enjoyed by all ages.

> Bring the water to a boil. Reduce the heat, add the herbs, and allow to simmer for 15 minutes. Remove from the heat and allow to steep for 15 minutes. Strain. Add honey and lemon juice to taste. Drink while still warm.

Easy Tonic Broth

Quick to assemble, this healthy broth brings together ingredients that are staples of a pantry well stocked for making wise concoctions. Shiitake mushrooms enhance the immune system and in Chinese medicine are valued for their ability to strengthen *qi*, vital life force or energy. Kombu, a dried sea vegetable, is rich in nutrients and minerals. Carrots, high in beta-carotene, an antioxidant that fights free radicals (see page 62) have also been shown to reduce blood cholesterol levels. Garlic, too, boosts the immune system and lowers cholesterol and blood pressure while protecting the liver. A paste made from fermented soybeans, miso helps ward off toxins and pollutants from the environment.

> **Combine all of the ingredients and bring to a boil. Reduce the heat, cover, and allow to simmer for 15 minutes. Strain and drink the broth while still hot. The broth can be served with brown rice, barley, or udon noodles for a more filling dish.**

MAKES 8 CUPS

8 cups purified water

6 dried or 8 fresh shiitake mushrooms with stems intact

2 pieces kombu

1 carrot, sliced

6 cloves minced garlic

1 tablespoon white miso

Green Tea

MAKES 1 CUP

1 heaping teaspoon genmaicha
tea leaves

1 cup purified water

The Japanese drink green tea daily and benefit from its many
healthful qualities. A proven antioxidant (see page 62) as well as
a general tonic for the entire system, green tea is also good for
the heart because it helps to lower cholesterol levels. In my experience, it energizes and provides mental clarity without the jar-
ring effects and potential gastrointestinal hazards of coffee.
Perhaps, it's the small amount of caffeine in green tea, but I like
to think that it's the centuries of inner wisdom contained in
each fragrant cup. No matter the reason, each morning at sun-
rise I brew some green tea in a well-seasoned iron teapot and
allow its magic to gently bring my thoughts into focus. My
favorite is genmaicha, or "popcorn" tea, because of the mellow,
nutty flavor that kernels of golden puffed rice add to the slightly
acrid tea leaves.

> **Bring the water to a bare boil. Remove from the heat.
Pour the water over the tea leaves and allow to infuse for 2
to 3 minutes. Strain and drink hot.**

Everybody's Healing and Nutritional Tea

RESISTANCE

Catherine Hunziker MacMann, herbalist and proprietor of Wishgarden Herbs in Boulder, Colorado, came up with this harmonious blend. When infused, the combination of herbs, berries, and roots makes a wonderful tea that acts as a tonic to the whole system. Nettles are high in iron and other minerals as well as vitamin C, which helps their absorption into your body. Alfalfa leaf, dubbed the father of all foods by the Arabs, is rich in protein. Red clover is a relaxant that has been used as an anticancer remedy since the 1930s. Hawthorn berries act as a tonic for the heart. Oatstraw is a restorative tonic and counteracts nervous and physical exhaustion while benefiting menopausal women with estrogen deficiencies. Dandelion root stimulates and cleanses the liver. Spearmint promotes good digestion and also has anti-inflammatory properties.

> **To make the herbal blend, combine the herbs and mix well. Store in an airtight container.**

MAKES ABOUT 3/4 CUP
HERBAL BLEND

2 tablespoons dried nettle leaves

2 tablespoons dried alfalfa leaves

2 tablespoons red clover blossoms

2 tablespoons hawthorn berries

2 tablespoons oatstraw

2 tablespoons dandelion root

2 tablespoons dried spearmint leaves

HERBAL TEA

> **To make the tea, bring the water to a boil and pour over herbal blend. Allow to steep for 20 minutes. Strain and drink while hot. Drink I to 3 cups a day.**

MAKES ABOUT I CUP

1 cup purified water

1 teaspoon Herbal Blend

Nam Singh's Nutritious Jook

MAKES 10 CUPS

10 cups water or chicken or vegetable stock

½ cup white rice

⅓ cup foxnuts

⅓ cup pearl barley

2 cups fresh corn (cut from the cob)

Salt or tamari

Jook, or congee, is a staple of Chinese cooking. Often eaten for breakfast as a porridge, it forms the basis for endless additions such as a poached egg, roasted peanuts, and seafood. Herbalists who practice Chinese medicinal cooking add herbs to various grains to create tonic jooks. The distinguishing technique used for cooking jook is the disproportionate amount of liquid to grain. In order to end up with a thin gruel or loose soup, eight to ten parts water are combined with one part grain, which is cooked on a very slow simmer for a longer time. Nam Singh, my teacher and good friend, created this light, tonic jook that is easy on the digestive system and effective in the summertime when fresh corn is at its peak. Corn helps increase urine flow to cleanse the kidneys; according to Chinese medicine, moving water through the body is especially important in summer. The grains also help urine flow, and barley acts as a decongestant. Foxnuts (*Euryale ferox*), available in Chinese groceries or by mail order, invigorate the vital energy of the kidneys. To make a similar jook in winter, adzuki beans can be substituted for the corn.

> **Bring the water or stock to a boil. Add the remaining ingredients, including salt or tamari to taste, and cook over a low simmer for at least 1 hour, stirring often so the grains do not stick to the bottom of the pot, until the jook has a porridge-like consistency. (The jook can also be made in a crockpot. If using chicken stock, bring the stock to a boil first before adding to the crockpot.) You can prepare the jook at night and allow it to cook on a bare simmer for eight hours so that it's ready for breakfast the next morning. Eat while still hot.**

Rose Hips Lemonade

MAKES 2 CUPS

1 cup purified water

½ teaspoon dried rose hips

½ teaspoon dried hibiscus flowers

1 cup fresh lemonade or orange juice

1 lemon slice

All of the ingredients in this cooling, earthy refreshment originate from flowers and fruit and contain healthy quantities of vitamin C. Used as a preventative tonic, the beverage provides a concentrated dose of antioxidants (see page 62) in liquid form. Think of this drink as a potent and elegant way to get your Cs and boost your immune system.

> **Bring the water to a boil. Pour over the rose hips and hibiscus flowers. Allow to steep for 15 minutes and then cool to room temperature. Combine well with the lemonade or orange juice and serve cold over ice or refrigerated. Garnish with the lemon slice.**

Orange Peel Tonic

Derived from an old folk recipe, this tonic promotes vigorous good health through its concentration of vitamin C. Vitamin C, of course, has become well known for its antioxidant powers (see page 62) and, when taken in large quantities, for its ability to help fend off the miseries of a cold. If you include the white of the peel in this tonic, you will also benefit from the bioflavonoids (see page 62), which help the body to more efficiently assimilate vitamin C. Orange Peel Tonic is one of the easiest tonics to make, and when paired with the spicy taste of cloves, it offers a pleasant change from the ubiquitous glass of orange juice.

> **Remove the peel from the orange and dice. Place in a mason jar or other container with a lid. Add the cloves and honey. Bring the water to a boil, pour in the jar, and stir slightly. Cover and allow to steep for 12 hours. Stir the tonic, cover again, and let stand for another 12 hours. Strain the tonic and drink at room temperature.**

MAKES 1 CUP

1 orange, preferably organic

3 whole cloves

1 teaspoon local honey

1 cup purified water

73

Seeds of Life Gel

Another contribution from Ed Bauman, this gel has become a staple in my refrigerator. It is a unique and simple way to enjoy the sustenance contained in seeds. According to Ed, seeds are nature's most nutrient-rich food, the essence of all the bounty that we enjoy from the plant kingdom. Frequently discarded when we make juice or eat whole fruits or vegetables, seeds nourish and enrich. A tablespoon of flax, sesame, sunflower, or pumpkin seeds can be added to salads, cooked cereals, blended drinks, salad dressings, soups, or cookies and desserts. Use the gel as a topping on cereal, yogurt, or pancakes, or spread on toast.

> Place the seeds, fruit, and spice (if using) in a glass container with a lid. Pour in the juice and soak overnight in the refrigerator. The mixture will congeal, just like gelatin. It keeps refrigerated for one week, but you'll find it won't last that long.

MAKES 1 CUP

4 tablespoons toasted
flax seeds,
whole or ground

2 tablespoons chia or sesame
seeds

2 tablespoons raisins or
chopped dried figs

½ teaspoon ground cardamom
or ground cinnamon (optional)

1 cup black cherry or apple-
berry juice

Summer Booster Blend

RESISTANCE

MAKES ABOUT 4 CUPS

2 to 3 cups organic
strawberries (see The Herbal
Pantry, page 110)

2 bananas

1 to 2 cups purified water

½ lemon

6 to 8 oranges or 1 cup of juice

1 tablespoon brewer's yeast
(optional)

2 teaspoons spirulina

Rich in antioxidant vitamins (see page 62) and bioflavonoids (see page 62), which enhance the immune system, this drink offers a delicious way to prevent summer colds. Strawberries are loaded with vitamins C and A, along with trace amounts of iron and potassium. Oranges and lemons are rich in bioflavonoids and have a rejuvenating effect if you eat the white pith and add a bit of the peel to the juice. Terpene, the phytochemical found in citrus fruit, helps cleanse the lymphatic system of potential toxins, allowing it to do its work building white blood cells to combat disease. The potassium in bananas plays a significant role in controlling blood pressure, and their fiber helps lower blood cholesterol. Protein, amino acids, minerals, and vitamins, which all strengthen the immune system, are added to this healthful drink, by the tablespoon of nutritional yeast. The spirulina contributes more protein and has a restorative effect on the body.

> Most of this drink can be made ahead and frozen to have on hand for a rushed morning wake-up drink. Blend the strawberries, bananas, and $^{1}/_{2}$ cup of the water in a blender. Pour the mixture into ice cube trays and freeze. Remove the zest from the lemon, and save for another use, leaving the pith just under the skin. Blend the lemon with $^{1}/_{2}$ cup water. Pour this mixture into another ice cube tray and freeze. When ready to make the blend, juice the oranges. Put the juice into a blender with the frozen cubes, nutritional yeast, and spirulina. Blend until smooth.

Supersonic Tonic

This bracing tonic is a lively interplay of delicate and emphatic flavors with benefits for several internal systems. The ginger is warming and stimulates the heart and circulatory system. Cayenne is rich in vitamin C, is antibacterial, and improves circulation. The astringent qualities of lemon help tissues to contract and release mucous so the system can be cleansed of toxins. It also provides additional vitamin C, an antioxidant. Lavender acts as a calming tonic for the nervous system. The honey makes it all go down a little easier and offsets the intensity of the cayenne and ginger. A drink for the adventurous spirit in search of a potent, multipurpose tonic.

> **Bring the water to a boil and cool slightly. Combine the ginger and lavender flowers. Add the hot water and allow to steep for 10 minutes. Strain and add the lemon juice, honey, and cayenne pepper. Stir well and sip slowly.**

MAKES 2 ½ CUPS

2 ½ cups purified water

1-inch piece fresh ginger root, peeled and grated or finely chopped

1 tablespoon dried or 2 tablespoons fresh lavender flowers, chopped

Juice from 1 lemon

2 tablespoons honey

⅛ teaspoon cayenne pepper

System Boosters

When our various internal systems function in harmony, we generally feel buoyant, at ease, and alert. Keeping them in good working order is crucial to our sense of well-being. These tonics boost individual system functions in several ways. Some clean out unwanted toxins from our kidneys and liver, two organs of elimination whose smooth functioning occupies a hallowed place in Traditional Chinese Medicine. Others strengthen the cardiovascular system by stimulating circulation and providing antioxidants (see page 62). Two recipes in this chapter fortify the digestive system with ingredients that prevent sluggishness and facilitate absorption of the nutrients available in food. Important female reproductive needs are addressed by a tisane using herbs that are hormone regulators.

Heart Health Tonic

MAKES 2 CUPS

1 cup freshly squeezed orange juice or orange juice concentrate

1 cup tomato juice

5 tablespoons wheat germ oil

1 tablespoon brewer's yeast

This blend can be used as a nonherbal alternative to nourish and strengthen the heart. The wheat germ oil is filled with vitamin E, which acts as an effective antioxidant. The folic acid in orange juice lowers the levels of an amino acid in the blood known to increase the risk of heart disease. The antioxidant properties of vitamin C are an additional benefit. Tomato juice also serves as a good source of vitamin C and vitamin A. The brewer's yeast is rich in B vitamins.

> **Combine all of the ingredients in a blender and mix on high speed until the brewer's yeast is thoroughly incorporated. Serve cold or at room temperature.**

Bladder Tonic Decoction

While some of the herbs in this decoction (see page 16) may sound less familiar than the cranberry concentrate that is more commonly recommended for the bladder and urinary tract, this root and herbal combination proves itself to be even more effective as a purifying tonic. The herbs are available through natural food markets or by mail order (see Resource Guide, page 116), and the decoction is quite easy to make. Uva ursi strengthens the kidney and bladder. Rose hips, high in vitamin C, flush the system and cleanse toxins from the blood. Peony root relieves congestion and, according to Chinese medicine, moves *qi* to the bladder area. Burdock root tonifies the liver and purifies the blood. Marshmallow root reduces bacterial growth by increasing the acid content of urine.

> Bring the water to a boil. Add the herbs and continue to boil for 5 minutes. Add the cranberry concentrate. Reduce the heat and simmer for 15 minutes. Strain and drink 2 to 3 cups three times a day.

MAKES 6 CUPS

6 cups purified water

1 teaspoon uva ursi

2 teaspoons dried rose hips

1 teaspoon peony root

1 teaspoon burdock root

1 teaspoon marshmallow root

1 teaspoon cranberry concentrate

Bouillon aux Herbes

Michel Pierre, the proprietor and master herbalist of the renowned Herboristerie du Palais-Royal in Paris, highly recommends this bouillon as a digestive tonic. On my last visit to his inspiring herbal emporium, I left with a sack full of his unique and very wise concoctions as well as his permission to share this recipe. As he describes in his book, *Au Bonheur des plantes*, the healing properties of bouillon historically have been an important part of France's medical arsenal. Based on old, established principles of slow cooking at very low temperatures in order to extract the medicinal properties, this particular folk recipe used to be called "tisane composed of sorrel" and according to Monsieur Pierre "refreshes and restores the digestive organs."

> **Combine the water and herbs and bring to a bare simmer. Cook, covered, for 2 hours. Add the salt and butter, if desired. Allow the butter to melt. Strain and sip while hot.**

MAKES 6 CUPS

6 cups purified water

½ cup chopped fresh sorrel

¼ cup chopped fresh lettuce

2 tablespoons chopped fresh chervil

2 tablespoons chopped leeks

Pinch of salt (optional)

1 teaspoon butter (optional)

Herbal Espresso

The popularity of espresso drinks in recent years and the frustration of friends who can't drink caffeinated beverages, but still yearn for the aroma and taste of freshly brewed coffee, led to the creation of Herbal Espresso. This delicious healthful blend comes close to the taste of the real thing and delivers a powerful tonic effect at the same time. Dandelion root has a reputation as a blood builder and liver strengthener, unlike coffee, which actually irritates the liver. The dark color and richness of chicory evoke the blended coffees of New Orleans. The tradition of adding chicory to coffee actually originated with the French, who believe this root counteracts the acidic quality of coffee. They also make chicory into a decoction on its own to neutralize stomach acidity. Ginseng, an overall tonic, acts as a natural stimulant for those who relish the energizing effect that coffee provides. Molasses contributes natural B vitamins and sweetness to replace refined sugar. Carob powder and cinnamon add aromatic flavorings.

> To make the espresso, bring the water to a boil. Place 3 to 5 teaspoons herb blend in a drip coffee filter. Pour the boiling water through the mixture and allow to drip into a coffee cup. Add the cinnamon and carob powder for added flavor. If too strong add more hot water. Sweeten to taste with molasses, honey, or maple syrup.

continues . . .

MAKES 1 TO 2 CUPS

1 to 2 cups purified water

3 to 5 teaspoons Herbal Espresso Blend (page 84)

½ teaspoon carob powder

1 to 2 teaspoons molasses, honey, or pure maple syrup

Pinch of ground cinnamon

83

HERBAL ESPRESSO BLEND

MAKES 1½ CUPS
HERB BLEND

1 cup dried chopped
chicory root

¼ cup dried chopped
dandelion root

¼ cup pearl barley

⅛ cup chopped ginseng
root (see Note)

> To make the herb blend, roast the chicory, dandelion, barley, and ginseng in a 200°F preheated oven for 2 hours. (Or roast in a large heavy skillet over medium heat for 10 minutes, stirring occasionally.) Grind in a clean coffee grinder until very fine. Store in a glass container with a lid.

NOTE: Ginseng is not recommended for pregnant women or individuals with high blood pressure. It may also have estrogenic activity, which aggravates fibrocystic breast disease in women. If any of these conditions are present, simply eliminate the ginseng from this mixture.

Herbal Latte

MAKES 2 CUPS

1 cup Herbal Espresso
(page 83)

1 cup soy milk

1 to 2 teaspoons molasses,
pure maple syrup, or honey

Pinch of ground cinnamon,
or more if desired

½ teaspoon carob powder,
or more if desired

This recipe embellishes Herbal Espresso if you prefer a foamy, milky hot drink. It combines the restorative qualities of Herbal Espresso with the additional preventative benefits of soy milk.

> Brew Herbal Espresso as directed. Steam the soy milk in an espresso steamer or saucepan until frothy. Fill a mug half full of espresso. Add the steaming hot milk. Stir in the molasses, maple syrup, or honey; cinnamon; and carob powder. Sprinkle with more carob powder or cinnamon, if desired.

Kidney-Liver Tonic

Before you toss the greens attached to a bunch of beets, read further. Those long, unglamorous leaves have powerful detoxifying properties for both the kidneys and the liver. Along with the carrots, apple, and whole beet in this tonic, they help the liver to filter the blood and remove impurities and toxins. Although this is an effective system cleanser after you have been on medication for infections, it's best to wait and use this recipe when your digestive system has calmed, as beets sometimes worsen a queasy stomach. This tonic can be followed with an infusion of raspberry leaf, which acts as an antidote to nausea. Simply pour I cup boiling water over I teaspoon dried raspberry leaf and steep for IO minutes.

> **Juice all ingredients and stir to mix well.**

MAKES I½ CUPS

2 to 3 carrots

1 apple, seeded

1 beet

4 beet greens

Kidney-Liver Support Decoction

This decoction is useful for cleansing the kidneys. Go easy on the fresh parsley, which is a diuretic that promotes the excretion of urine and can cleanse the kidneys too fast, causing them to ache. Make a decoction (see page I6) with the following ingredients and drink I to 2 cups.

> **Bring the water to a boil. Add the herbs and continue to boil for 5 minutes. Steep for 20 minutes. Strain and drink warm.**

MAKES 4 CUPS

4 cups purified water

1 tablespoon chopped fresh parsley

1 tablespoon burdock root

Metabolic Tonic

SYSTEM BOOSTERS

MAKES 2¹/₂ CUPS

5 cinnamon sticks, broken in half

2 half-inch slices fresh ginger root

½ teaspoon cardamom seeds

⅛ teaspoon whole cloves

3 cups purified water

A restorative that enlivens the metabolism by creating heat and energy, this tonic stimulates circulation. Its warming ingredients are particularly recommended for winter chills. The warming quality of cinnamon works well when paired with ginger as a preventative as well as for conditions related to poor circulation such as cold hands and feet. Cardamom, in addition to its warmth, adds nourishment and energy. Cloves stimulate the digestion.

> **Combine all the ingredients and simmer until the tonic reduces slightly. Strain and drink hot or iced.**

Nourishing Chewy Tonic

MAKES 1¹/₂ CUPS

1 or 2 apples, seeded

1 cup chopped fresh pineapple or canned pineapple chunks with juice

6 kale, spinach, chard, or dandelion leaves

Drink this juice a half hour before, or one hour after, meals to aid digestion. Be sure to "chew" the juice, swishing each sip around in your mouth for increased absorption of its nutrients, as if tasting an exquisite Bordeaux. Liquid chlorophyll, produced in the leaves of green plants by the sun, is an excellent source of minerals and vitamins. Pineapple is rich in manganese, which fights fatigue, poor memory, nervous tension, and irritability and also contains bromelain, an enzyme that aids digestion. Apples, one of the healthiest foods for the heart, help lower blood cholesterol by reducing the absorption of fat.

> **Juice all the ingredients. Stir well to mix.**

Women's Balancing Tisane

The chasteberry in this tisane has been used for centuries as an effective female system regulator because it stimulates and normalizes hormone function by acting on the pituitary gland. Women experience a more balanced emotional state and a reduction in PMS and in menopausal symptoms when ingesting this fruit. Raspberry leaf is commonly used by women for menstrual cramps since it contains a phytochemical, fragine, that relaxes the smooth muscle of the uterus. It is also known as an excellent uterine strengthener and as a source of vitamins C, E, A, and B, as well as iron, calcium, and phosphorous.

> **Bring the water to a boil. Add the herbs and allow to steep for 5 minutes. Strain and drink warm.**

NOTE: IF DRIED CHASTEBERRIES ARE UNAVAILABLE, SUBSTITUTE 10 DROPS VITEX TINCTURE, WHICH IS AN EXTRACT OF THE BERRIES.

MAKES 4 CUPS

4 cups purified water

1 tablespoon chasteberry (see Note)

1 tablespoon raspberry leaf

Rejuvenation and Concentration

These following concoctions extend energy to the weary, clarity to the muddle-headed, and—at least in one instance—a promise of sexual ardor. Whether you choose to prepare the Ayurvedic Tridoshic Tea that combines fennel seeds with rose petals and gotu kola to help brighten the mind, or Margaret's Spicy Aphrodisiac with cardamom pods to kindle desire, you will most likely come upon ingredients you are sampling for the first time, or familiar herbs and spices used in new ways. Replenishment comes in many forms. Experimentation and discovery lie at the heart of the folk-recipe healthful beverage tradition. The recipes in this section are divided into two categories, mind and body stimulants, although in truth I've rarely come upon a rejuvenating beverage that didn't seem to accomplish both tasks at once.

Brain Blast

The brain, like any other organ in the body, can be stimulated and fortified. Some herbs are known for their ability to reinforce brain function, and the vitamins, minerals, and protein in certain foods can also ensure mental agility and alertness. Kelp is a natural source of iodine, which stimulates brain activity and impedes the accumulation of plaque, which can clog the arteries. Apricots are rich in beta-carotene as well as minerals such as potassium and calcium. Lecithin, a soy by-product, boosts mental and nervous system functions and adds smoothness to this foamy drink.

> **Combine all the ingredients in a blender until well mixed and smooth. If desired, add 1 or 2 ice cubes and blend well.**

MAKES 2 1/2 CUPS

1 teaspoon freshly squeezed lemon juice

½ teaspoon kelp

1½ cups apricot juice

1 cup soy milk

1 tablespoon lecithin

Tridoshic Tea

Herbalist Amadea Morningstar, who created this recipe, explains that it is calming and strengthening. Gotu kola helps brighten the mind and brings clarity while relaxing the nervous system, which makes it a preferred herb for meditators. (It should not be used in excess as it can cause headaches and itching if you have a predisposition to either condition.) The spearmint and fennel flavor the tea and also calm the digestive tract, while the rose petals add sweet, cooling, and soothing elements to this herbal blend.

> **Bring the water to a boil. Remove from the heat and stir in the herbs. Steep for 10 minutes, strain, and serve.**

MAKES 4 CUPS

4 cups purified water

1 tablespoon dried gotu kola leaves

1 tablespoon dried spearmint leaves

⅛ teaspoon fennel seeds

1 tablespoon dried organic rose petals

Bauman Vitality Broth

MAKES 8 CUPS

3 to 4 cups cubed winter squash such as butternut or delicata, plus seeds from squash

2 cups cubed yams

4 or 5 new red potatoes

4 beets

5 carrots

1 to 2 onions, sliced

8 cups purified water

½ cup wakame or hijiki

2 tablespoons flax seeds

4 beet greens

3 dandelion greens

3 Swiss chard or kale leaves

Potassium, a vital mineral that regulates water balance, is easily depleted in your system by consuming coffee, alcohol, and sugar, and through excessive perspiration, vomiting, or diarrhea. Potassium deficiency can result in fatigue, depression, muscle weakness, and slow or irregular heartbeat. This broth, created by nutritionist Ed Bauman of the Institute for Educational Therapy, includes vegetables and seeds rich in potassium and vitamins C, A, and E, as well as selenium, zinc, folic acid, magnesium, calcium, and iron. The hijiki, like wakame, a nutrient-rich sea vegetable, is high in protein and calcium, which strengthen the bones, intestines, skin, and hair. In addition to calcium, the wakame also contains thiamin, niacin, and vitamin B-12, which makes it an excellent blood purifier that strengthens the intestines and reproductive organs and helps regulate menstrual cycles. An exquisite, sweet broth that replenishes the body.

> Soak the winter squash, yams, potatoes, beets, and carrots in water to cover for 15 minutes with the skins intact. (They are rich in bioflavonoids and other phytochemicals, which boost the immune system.) Drain and cut the soaked vegetables and the onions into chunks. Combine with the water and bring to a boil. Reduce the heat and simmer 2 to 3 hours. Add the wakame or hijiki, seeds, and greens, and simmer for an additional 30 minutes. Strain. Drink 2 to 4 cups a day. Because of its sweetness, it's delicious in the morning.

Sage Focus Tisane

MAKES 1 CUP

1 cup purified water

2 teaspoons fresh or 1 teaspoon dried sage leaves (see Note)

Honey

Sage has a long-standing reputation as a longevity herb as well as a memory enhancer. For that reason, the Chinese were willing to swap two cases of tea for every one of English sage during the early days of the British tea trade. In the sixteenth century, one English herbalist, Gerard, cited its powers: "Sage is singularly good for head and brain, it quickeneth the senses and memory . . ." During the nineteenth century, it became the most popular dried herb sold by the Shakers. In fact, scientists have since discovered that sage provides oxygen to the brain's cortex to revitalize brain power and improve concentration. Since the herb is easily grown in many parts of the world and is a staple of most kitchen herb gardens, the benefits in a cup of sage tea are easily accessible to all of us.

> **Bring the water to a boil. Pour over the sage and allow to steep for 5 minutes. Strain and add honey to taste. Drink warm, as often as needed.**

NOTE: Large quantities of sage should not be taken during pregnancy. It should also be avoided by epileptics.

Energy Buzzer

MAKES 3 1/2 CUPS

2 cups freshly squeezed
orange juice

1 cup vanilla yogurt or vanilla
soy milk

1 banana

1 teaspoon bee pollen

3 dates, pitted

The recipe for this enlivening cold beverage has evolved over the years from its origins as "Golden Cow," a nourishing drink I used to make for my children when they were young. The original ingredients were orange juice, yogurt, and bananas with some honey to sweeten it. In its current incarnation as a wise concoction, the recipe replaces honey with iron-rich dates and provides the option of using soy milk. Bee pollen boosts energy and stamina while adding a slightly crunchy texture to this vitalizing shake.

> Blend all ingredients thoroughly in a blender. If you prefer a chilled drink, add an ice cube and blend on high until it has been completely crushed.

Healing Virgin Mary

You don't have to wait for the cocktail hour to be energized by this healthy, nonalcoholic drink. Rich in minerals and vitamins, it renews and rejuvenates. At the same time, it nourishes your body with the iron, vitamins A and C, potassium, magnesium, calcium, and folic acid found in all of the vegetables. Try it for breakfast if you want to eliminate caffeine. The cayenne may be all the jump-start you really need.

> **Juice two of the celery stalks and the spinach, tomatoes, bell peppers, and parsley. Pour into a blender and add the cayenne, Worcestershire sauce, and lemon juice to taste. Add salt to taste. Blend until smooth. Garnish with the remaining celery stick.**

MAKES 2 CUPS

3 celery stalks

2 spinach leaves

3 tomatoes

½ red bell pepper

½ green bell pepper

1 tablespoon chopped fresh parsley

Pinch of cayenne pepper

1 teaspoon Worcestershire sauce

Freshly squeezed lemon juice

Salt

Live Culture Tonic

MAKES 4 CUPS

1 cup soft wheat berries or
any whole grain, such as
millet or barley

Purified water

1½ tablespoons fresh lemon
juice

1 teaspoon honey

Originally developed by Ann Wigmore of Hippocrates Health Institute and adapted here for more pleasure on the palate, this is an excellent restorative tonic that is often served in health spas. The fermented liquid, known as Rejuvelac, contains friendly bacteria, enzymes, and vitamins B, C, and E. Live lactobacilli culture, actually beneficial flora, helps maintain intestinal heath, and its high vitamin E content makes it a natural antioxidant. For increased energy and as a digestive aid, you can drink this tonic at least once a week. Because of the fermentation, it will look a bit cloudy and have a tangy taste. Think of it as an easily absorbed multivitamin.

> Pour the grain and 4 cups purified water into a wide-mouth mason jar. Cover with a 6-inch square of cheesecloth and use a thick rubber band to secure the cheesecloth over the mouth of the jar. Soak the grain for 8 to 10 hours. Drain the water through the cheesecloth and rinse the grain with purified water. Put the jar at an angle to allow for drainage, making sure the grains do not cover the mouth of the jar. The grain will begin to sprout within 2 days. Rinse twice daily.

> Once the sprouts appear, add 4 more cups purified water and soak for another 24 hours (or up to 48 hours for a tangier taste.) Strain the liquid and reserve. To serve, blend 1 cup of the liquid with lemon juice and honey. The remaining liquid will keep in the refrigerator for several days. You can use the berries or grains to make 2 more batches. Just add 4 cups purified water and soak for 24 hours again.

Long Life Tonic

MAKES 2 1/2 CUPS

3 cups purified water

1 cup dried longan berries

2 cups lycii berries

1 cup mulberries

⅓ plus ¼ cup brandy

The sweetness of the berries in this tonic, prescribed by herbalist Nam Singh, helps strengthen the spleen, which in Traditional Chinese Medicine is often referred to as the pilot light of the digestive system. A fortified spleen keeps our internal energy flow, or *qi*, in good working order, ready to function as needed. "Vital clear" is the expression for this state of readiness. The tonic also invigorates circulation and counteracts sluggishness. Its alcohol content extracts the medicinal properties from the berries and acts as a catalyst, allowing them to enter the bloodstream faster. The longan increases blood flow and stimulates the spleen *qi*. Lycii berries nourish the blood, liver, and eyes, and the mulberries support the kidneys and liver, tonify the blood, eliminate gas, and prevent insomnia. When you drink this tonic, you will feel a sustained warmth that slowly dissipates and leaves you with a "golden glow" of health.

> Bring the water to a boil. As soon as it boils, add the longan berries, lycii berries, and mulberries and immediately turn off the heat. Allow to stand for 5 minutes. Add the ⅓ cup brandy. Cover and steep until the mixture cools. The berries will absorb some of the water. Strain, gently pressing the berry sludge without breaking it up. (You can eat this fruit as a dessert on its own or as an accompaniment to custards. It will last up to 2 weeks when refrigerated.) Warm the ¼ cup brandy. Add to the tonic. Refrigerate for up to 1 month. Take 1 tablespoon three times a day, preferably on an empty stomach.

Natural Aphrodisiacs

Where would Casanova be without his chocolates, or Solomon without those pomegranates that lured women to hear his song of songs? Standing on the corner watching all the girls go by, probably. The pomegranate, which appears in carvings on King Solomon's temple, is called in biblical Hebrew *rimmon*, which means "to bear offspring." Its juice was long consumed by women as a fertility tonic. The Mayans used cacao as currency in brothels, and Montezuma of the Aztecs sipped a chocolate brew in golden goblets before an evening with his concubines. Even vanilla, whose name comes from the Latin word for vagina, was employed by Louis XV's mistress to keep her lovers ready and eager.

Other foods and herbs also belong in the passionate pantry. The South Pacific plant kava-kava acts as a mild sedative; its root is sometimes blended into a "love cocktail" that supposedly reduces inhibition. At the other extreme—energy and endurance—the bark extract yohimbe has for centuries been used in Africa to prolong lovemaking and increase physical feelings of arousal.

Not to be left out of this intimate conversation, of course, is our most advanced erogenous zone, the mind. Down through the ages, the world's greatest lovers have understood the seductive power of the imagination and have appealed to it in music, art, and poetry. As a result we have inherited not only a complete library of love-potion recipes, but a deluge of aphrodisiac lore as well, dating long before Aphrodite's emergence from the foam in Greek mythology.

As for proof—well, chocolate has recently been discovered to contain an amino acid that increases sexual arousal—but do you really want to occupy your mind with that? Better, perhaps, to accept that most lovers prefer to be left in the dark with their liquid refreshments.

Margaret's Spicy Aphrodisiac

MAKES 4 CUPS

4 cups purified water

1 tangerine, peel intact, sliced

3 cardamom pods, split open

1-inch piece fresh ginger root, sliced

Dash of ground nutmeg

½ vanilla bean or 1 teaspoon pure vanilla extract

4 cinnamon sticks

1 to 2 teaspoons pomegranate seeds

New York herbalist Margaret Dexter was kind enough to share this aphrodisiac recipe. Personal discretion prevents me from discussing my own reaction to it, but the ingredients certainly speak for themselves. Ginger, tangerine, pomegranate, and nutmeg are all natural stimulants and thus, according to folklore, evoke an aphrodisiac effect. Vanilla also has a long history of "love-heightening" effects. Margaret claims this is one of her favorite and most requested recipes. Once you try it and light a few well-placed candles, you'll understand why.

> **Combine all the ingredients except two of the cinnamon sticks and the pomegranate seeds. Simmer, covered, for 20 minutes, stirring occasionally. Add the pomegranate seeds for the last 5 minutes. Remove from the heat. Serve in your most tactile cups with a cinnamon stick in each for stirring.**

Sexual Vigor Tonic

Not intended as an aphrodisiac, this tonic tea instead promotes sexual vigor by replenishing spent energy. According to Traditional Chinese Medicine, whenever energy is expended, it must be replaced to maintain overall balance and vibrant health. The orchid helps restore lost body fluids and the licorice invigorates the body.

> **Combine all the ingredients and bring to a boil. Boil for 5 minutes. Reduce the heat and simmer, uncovered, for 30 minutes. Strain and drink while still hot.**

MAKES 4 1/2 CUPS

5 cups purified water

2 cups Chinese orchid

5 pieces Chinese licorice root

Postworkout Broth

Whether you break a sweat on a vigorous hike or on a treadmill at the gym, the ingredients in this broth help to maintain potassium levels and replenish your mineral electrolytes, crucial to efficient cell function. It also restores energy if you have stayed out in the sun too long. The high concentration of potassium in these three vegetables also helps maintain cellular function and prevents dehydration. Prepare the broth ahead of time so that it is ready after your workout.

> **Combine the vegetables and water, and bring to a boil. Reduce the heat and simmer, covered, for 45 to 50 minutes. Strain and refrigerate if using after your workout. Heat the broth and sip while still warm.**

MAKES 8 CUPS

2 cups grated carrots

2 cups grated potatoes

2 cups grated yams

8 cups purified water

Cleansing

In the best of all worlds, we'd be eating only healthy foods and breathing nothing but pure air. Few of us are that fortunate, of course. After a day of empty-calorie foods, secondhand smoke, exhaust emissions, and work stress, our minds and bodies often need tender loving care, and cleansing tonics are an excellent way to receive it. As we sip and enjoy a vegetable juice that helps detoxify the liver and gall bladder, or try a homemade root beer that works to purify the blood (instead of grabbing a soft drink), we return equilibrium to our systems. After a winter's diet rich in protein and heavier, fatty foods, it is especially important to cleanse and rejuvenate the system. Highly recommended in this process are foods with a high chlorophyll content, such as dandelion leaves, which act as a powerful liver detoxifier while providing nourishment to the intestines.

In this crucial cleansing process, I have particularly come to trust the beneficial properties of sea vegetables. They bond with environmental pollutants to speed their elimination from the body, and they also happen to be delicious when correctly prepared.

Spring Cleaning Tonic

A plentiful source of chlorophyll as well as vitamins and minerals, this tonic nurtures and restores. Also known as the "green drink," it is best made in spring, when the plants are young and fresh. At that time of year, as our thoughts turn to renewal, it cleanses the body of winter's accumulation of toxins from heavy foods. If you don't feel confident about identifying and gathering fresh herbs on your own, you can find them in abundance in farmers' markets and natural food stores beginning in early spring. You also might consider planting an herb garden so that herbal seasonings and ingredients are readily available by simply walking out the back door with pruning shears in hand. Feel free to substitute other leafy herbs for those listed here, and create your own version of this nourishing blend.

> **Place all the ingredients in a blender and blend on high speed until the leaves are liquefied. Allow to stand for a few minutes and strain.**

MAKES 4 CUPS

2 handfuls mixed fresh herbs: parsley, dandelion leaves, mint, chickweed, miner's lettuce, nettles, or plantain

4 cups pineapple juice or freshly squeezed orange juice

1 teaspoon freshly squeezed lemon juice

Gladiator Tonic

MAKES 1 1/2 CUPS

2 carrots, cut into chunks

1 small beet, cut into chunks

2 apples, seeded and cut into chunks

1 to 2 cups watercress (see Note)

2 to 3 dandelion leaves

1 tablespoon lecithin

This tonic juice is very effective in clearing toxins from the gall bladder and liver and reducing cholesterol. It usually follows that if the liver is congested, the gall bladder will also be affected since it stores the fat-digesting bile produced by the liver. Watercress, apples, and dandelion leaves are all rich in minerals and are excellent detoxifiers and blood purifiers. Carrots contribute fiber and are rich in carotenoids (these become vitamin A when digested), which act as antioxidants against free radicals (see page 62) and slow the rate at which LDL cholesterol (the "bad" cholesterol that can lead to heart disease through arterial plaque formation) affects the body. Lecithin, an important nutrient made from soy, helps to emulsify fats (which contain LDL cholesterol) so they can be eliminated through cell walls.

> Juice all of the vegetables and greens. Transfer the juice to a blender. Add the lecithin and blend until well mixed and frothy. Serve cold or at room temperature.

NOTE: BE SURE TO WASH THE WATERCRESS THOROUGHLY AS IT CAN HARBOR WORMS.

Sea Veggie Purification Broth

Sea vegetables such as nori, dulse, hijiki, kombu, and wakame not only taste and smell delicious, evoking flavors and scents of the ocean, but also provide a bounty of beneficial nutrients. Commonly used in sushi, salads, and broths, they prove to be rich in proteins, minerals, and antioxidants (see page 62). The Japanese, who have long been wise to their numerous advantages, frequently incorporate them into their diets. Sea vegetables can help strengthen our defenses against infections and environmental pollutants by bonding with them and moving them through the body until they are eliminated. This delicate broth, made with wakame, delivers ample protein as well as a good amount of iron, calcium, and sodium.

> Sauté the onions, carrot, ginger, and celery in the oil for 5 minutes. Remove from the heat. Rinse the wakame and cover with 2 cups of the water. Let stand for several minutes until it is just softened. (Don't allow it to soak too long or it will become too soft.) Discard the soaking water and cut the wakame into small pieces. Combine with the remaining 4 cups water and bring to a boil. Add the sautéed vegetables to the broth, reduce the heat, and simmer, covered, for 15 minutes. Drink while still warm or at room temperature.

MAKES 4 CUPS

4 green onions, chopped

1 carrot, chopped

½ inch piece fresh ginger root, peeled and chopped

2 celery stalks, chopped

1 tablespoon olive oil

4 pieces wakame

6 cups purified water

Roots "Beer"

MAKES 8 CUPS

4 cinnamon sticks

½ cup sassafras bark

½ cup sarsaparilla root

¼ cup burdock root

½ cup dried wintergreen leaves

1 tablespoon dried
orange peel

3 half-inch slices fresh
ginger root

1 vanilla bean

4 cups purified water

½ cup honey

4 cups carbonated mineral
water

Old-fashioned root beer conjures up images of Chevy Impala convertibles, drive-in movies, ice-cream floats, and lazy summer afternoons. But what was to become an all-American soft drink actually had its origins in Native American healing. The "roots" used to make authentic root beer have tonic properties that help purge toxins and nourish the system. Sassafras, sarsaparilla, and burdock root purify the blood. Wintergreen contains salicylates, or natural "aspirin," and adds its refreshing taste, while cinnamon and ginger are warming and stimulate circulation. Both vanilla and sarsaparilla are reputed to be aphrodisiacs, which may partially account for root beer's perennial popularity. For a healthier version of the traditional root beer float, try this with a scoop of vanilla frozen yogurt.

> **Combine the herbs, orange peel, ginger, and vanilla bean. Add the purified water and simmer, covered, for 15 minutes. Strain, add the honey, and stir well. Cool and then pour in the carbonated mineral water. Serve iced.**

The Herbal Pantry

Here is a brief description of the herbs used to make the recipes in this book. I urge you to explore the vast range of beneficial herbs that exists in today's marketplace to create your own wise concoctions. Always keep in mind that the highest quality and freshest herbs will produce the best results.

You will notice that throughout the book I have specified the use of purified water. By this I mean filtered water. There are numerous gadgets, at all prices, that remove potentially harmful deposits from your tap water; bottled filtered water can also be found on the supermarket shelf. In preparing these healthy brews, I consider it vital to use water that does not carry toxins or impart a chemical aftertaste.

The recent proliferation of organic fruits, vegetables, nuts, and soy products in mainstream markets allows you to eliminate the possibility of pesticide residue and other contaminants in these recipes. It is worth the extra effort and higher cost to seek them out in natural food markets if your supermarket does not stock them. This is especially important when using strawberries, since chemicals are easily absorbed into their soft skin. Unless the strawberries you use are certified organic, substitute another organically grown berry in the recipes that call for them. Once you have tasted fruit and vegetables grown without pesticides or inorganic fertilizers, you will never want any others. Be sure to scrub all vegetables and fruits before juicing or blending.

The cooking and brewing utensils you use also contribute to the success of the concoctions. It is best to avoid aluminum or other reactive cookware that can release chemicals when making the decoctions and broths. For some of the recipes, you will need a juicer. This has become a welcome addition to my kitchen that has paid back its expense many times over. Other recipes require a blender, which I have found to be more efficient than a food processor for making these drinks. All manner of crockery, from your grandmother's porcelain teapot to a contemporary handcrafted design, will certainly intensify your appreciation for the tisanes you steep in them. As mentioned in the Infusion Guide (page 16), earthenware or glass teapots are preferred. When making one cup, a stainless steel, wire mesh, or bamboo tea strainer and a favorite mug are all you will need.

Finally, I am sure you will find, as I have, that paying mindful attention to all of the ingredients you choose offers the immediate reward of enhanced flavor and effectiveness.

ALFALFA. Green plant that is a rich source of minerals and chlorophyll. Restorative to the whole system and an excellent spring tonic. Form: Dried leaves.

ALLSPICE. Aromatic herb reminiscent of nutmeg, cloves, and cinnamon that mixes well in warming spice blends. Reputed to aid digestion and ease flatulence. Form: Ground berries.

ANGELICA (DONG QUAI). Strong-smelling root related to celery, known as the "queen" of female herbs in Traditional Chinese Medicine. Nourishes the blood and regulates the menstrual cycle. Form: Ground dried root.

ASTRAGALUS. Root of the milk vetch plant, a popular herb in Traditional Chinese Medicine. Fortifies the immune system by increasing the production of white blood cells. Form: Shaved dried root.

BASIL. Pungent herb best recognized as a culinary virtuoso. Aids digestion and fatigue. Form: Fresh and dried leaves.

BLACK PEPPER. Fruit of a tall climbing shrub widely used as a food condiment. Acts as a digestive and counteracts nausea and constipation. Form: Ground dried fruit.

BURDOCK. Cooling, slightly sweet root vegetable. Traditionally used as a blood purifier and cleanser because of its antimicrobial effects. Form: Chopped dried root.

CARDAMOM. Aromatic spice with a slight peppery flavor. Helps stimulate digestion and improve the appetite. Form: Dried pods, whole or ground.

CAYENNE PEPPER. Versatile medicinal and culinary herb with a piquant taste. Offers tonic effects for the entire system and antibacterial actions. Form: Ground dried pod.

CHAMOMILE. Flavorful herb that yields a white-petaled flower with a yellow center and a slightly "appley" scent. Sedative and calming as well as promoting digestive actions. Form: Dried flowers.

CHASTEBERRY. Tiny, round berries of the chaste tree or shrub that grow on tall spikes (also known as vitex). Believed to regulate the pituitary functions and normalize hormones to alleviate PMS and menopausal symptoms. Form: Dried berries.

CHICORY ROOT. Long taproot of the blue-flowering chicory plant often used as a coffee substitute. A bitter tonic with diuretic effects and a good source of potassium. Form: Chopped dried root.

CHINESE ORCHID (SHI HU). Dendrobium orchid considered a tonic herb in Traditional Chinese Medicine. A kidney tonic that increases body fluids and also strengthens the lungs and stomach. Form: Dried stems.

CINNAMON. Pungent bark of the cinnamon plant, considered warming for colds and a good digestive ailment remedy. In Traditional Chinese Medicine a kidney tonic and energizing herb. Form: Rolled sticks of dried bark; ground dried bark.

DANDELION. Named for the shape of its leaf, which resembles a lion's tooth. All parts of this healthful plant have medicinal properties. The leaves and root detoxify and stimulate the liver and purify the blood. The leaves are also a diuretic. Form: Fresh leaves or chopped dried root.

DILL. Seeds of the dill plant, most often associated with pickles, vinegars, and breads. Effective to ease indigestion, flatulence, and colic. Form: Dried seeds.

ECHINACEA. One of the most highly regarded Native American herbs. An immune system stimulant that helps fight infection by increasing the production of white blood cells. Form: Chopped dried root.

ELDERFLOWERS. Delicate yellow flowers of the elder plant, once described as the "complete medicine chest." An antidote to colds and flu, they encourage sweating and counteract upper respiratory symptoms. Form: Fresh or dried flowers.

FENNEL. Seeds of the fennel plant that are often chewed after a meal to prevent upset stomach disorders. Calms digestion and colic. Form: Dried seeds.

FOXNUT. Mild-flavored Chinese herb related to lotus nuts used in fish and meat soups and as a tonic. Stimulates the energy of the kidney according to Traditional Chinese Medicine. Form: Nuts.

GARLIC. "Cure-all" perennial bulb with an ancient healing folklore tradition. Lowers blood cholesterol, helps in cardiovascular disease, and has antibacterial and antibiotic properties. Form: Cloves.

GINGER. Pungent rhizome of the ginger plant often used in Asian cuisine. A warming, multipurpose herb that invigorates the circulatory system, promotes good digestion, and remedies nausea. Form: Fresh or chopped dried root.

GINGKO BILOBA. Leaf of the maidenhair tree that has recently been the focus of media attention as a memory enhancer. Helps improve the circulation of blood to the brain and useful for circulatory diseases. Form: Dried leaves.

GINSENG. Considered a panacea for centuries, ginseng root is probably the most valued tonic herb. Replenishes spent energy, stimulates the appetite, and invigorates. Form: Chopped dried root.

GOTU KOLA. Plant that is part of the parsley family used in Ayurvedic medicine and as an aid for meditation. Clarifies the mind and relaxes the nervous system. Form: Dried leaves.

HAWTHORN. Fruit of the hawthorn tree known for its efficacy as a heart tonic. Slows the heartbeat and regulates blood pressure to prevent arteriosclerosis and angina pectoris. Form: Dried berries.

HIBISCUS. Lemon-flavored sepal of flowers of the tropical bush that is rich in vitamin C. Blends well with other herbs and is useful as an antioxidant. Form: Dried flowers.

HOREHOUND. Plant known for its healing properties since biblical times. Acts as an expectorant to expel mucous and as a decongestant. Form: Fresh or dried leaves.

KAVA KAVA. Root of a plant with origins in the South Seas, where it was made into a drink used during religious ceremonies. Calms the nervous system and has diuretic effects. Form: Dried root.

KOMBU, KELP, WAKAME, AND OTHER SEA VEGETABLES. Sea vegetables (seaweeds) are a potent source of beneficial health effects due to their exceptional nutritional makeup. Whole system nourishment from the minerals, protein, and vitamins plentiful in most seaweed. Form: Dried plants.

LAVENDER. Fragrant flower of a plant long valued as a healing herb. Calms, balances, and counteracts headaches and depression. Form: Dried or fresh flowers.

LEMON BALM. Fragrant citrusy leaves of the melissa plant used for centuries as a tonic and healing herb. Eases symptoms of stress such as anxiety and depression and digestive upset. Form: Fresh leaves (preferable) or dried leaves.

LEMON VERBENA. Leaves of the plant (a botanical relative of vervain) with a pure, citrus scent; can be infused as a tisane. Mildly sedative and a good digestive. Form: Fresh or dried leaves.

LICORICE. One of the most prevalent herbs in Traditional Chinese Medicine, but a different species than that used in Western medicine.

Benefits all the organs and balances the effects of other herbs. Form: Chopped dried root.

LINDEN OR LIMEFLOWER. Flowers of the linden (lime) tree are the basis for a favorite European tisane (tilleul). Promotes sweating in colds and calms nervous tension. Form: Dried flowers.

LONGAN. Berries of Euphoria longan used in Chinese healing herbal teas, soups, and confections. Nourishing to the blood and very effective for insomnia. Form: Dried berries.

LYCII (CHINESE WOLFBERRIES). Slightly sweet herb prevalent in traditional Chinese tonic soups and teas. Nourishing for the eyes and as a kidney and liver tonic. Form: Dried berries.

MARSHMALLOW. Used by herbalists to soothe inflammation because the root of the plant has a high mucilage content. Reduces inflammation in coughs and bacterial growth in the urinary tract. Form: Chopped dried root.

MINT (SPEARMINT AND PEPPERMINT). Both varieties of the plant are easily accessible and effective herbal treatments. Alleviates cold symptoms and aids digestion. Form: Fresh or dried leaves.

MULBERRY. Berries of the white mulberry mainly used in Traditional Chinese Medicine. Support kidney and liver function and nourish the blood. Form: Dried berries.

NETTLES. Plant that is often a nuisance to hikers because of its stinging leaves but is actually a powerful tonic, rich in vitamins and minerals. Full of vitamin C, stimulating to the circulatory system, and cleansing. Form: Dried leaves.

NUTMEG. Kernel of the plant, usually grated or ground, known for its aromatic, warming qualities. When used sparingly, remedies digestive ailments such as diarrhea, indigestion, and nausea. Form: Ground herb.

OATSTRAW. Whole oat plant that when dried and cut makes a soothing tonic herb. Restorative actions counteract fatigue and nervous exhaustion as well as estrogen deficiencies during menopause. Form: Dried plant.

PARSLEY. Best known as a culinary garnish and natural breath freshener, the leaves also have medicinal benefits. An effective antispasmodic for the digestion and a diuretic that flushes the bladder of toxins. Also rich in vitamin C. Form: Fresh (preferable) or dried leaves.

PASSIONFLOWER. Common and nonaddictive antidote for insomnia and anxiety, which mixes well with other sedative herbs. Calms the nervous system and acts as a sedative. Form: Dried flowers.

PEONY. Root of the plant is predominantly used in Traditional Chinese Medicine. Often prescribed for circulatory and menstrual difficulties. Form: Dried root.

RASPBERRY. Long-standing member of the herbal apothecary, the leaf of the plant has advantages for the female reproductive system. Uterine stimulant and diuretic. Form: Fresh or dried leaves.

RED CLOVER. Lightly fragrant flowers of the wild clover plant often used in tea blends. A relaxant that remedies coughs and bronchitis. Form: Dried blossoms.

RED DATES. Fruit of a shrub (zizyphus jujuba) used medicinally and in Chinese herbal cooking. Considered an energy tonic for the circulatory system. Form: Dried fruit.

ROSE. Petals of red roses (organically grown), which are slightly astringent (drying) and can be used for a delicate, sweet flavoring. Cooling and soothing. Form: Fresh or dried petals.

ROSE HIPS. Bulbous orange hips of the rose plant form highly concentrated packets of vitamin C. Antioxidant based on vitamin C content and also a remedy for diarrhea. Form: Fresh or dried hips.

ROSEMARY. Leaves of this highly aromatic shrub have a long association with "remembrance" or memory. Stimulate circulation and lift the spirit when depressed. Form: Fresh or dried leaves.

SAGE. Considered a sacred herb by the Romans, the leaf of the flowering sage plant also has numerous culinary uses. Increases circulation and acts as a blood and nervous system tonic. Aids digestion and contains estrogen. Form: Fresh or dried leaves.

SARSAPARILLA. Root of this trailing vine has traditionally been used as a soft-drink flavoring. A tonic herb that purifies the blood. Form: Chopped dried root.

SASSAFRAS. Bark, like that of sarsaparilla, has been used in soft drinks and as a tonic. A blood purifier that encourages sweating and a diuretic. Form: Dried bark.

SIBERIAN GINSENG. Root of the plant known for its ability to increase vitality. A tonic herb that energizes and invigorates but with less pronounced effects than Korean or American ginseng. Form: Dried root.

SKULLCAP. Leaves of the plant are an effective nervous system tonic. Calm the nerves and alleviate anxiety and insomnia. Form: Dried leaves.

SPIRULINA. Considered to be a "green superfood," this popular form of algae contains a high content of protein, B vitamins, beta-carotene, minerals, and essential fatty acids. Nutritious and energizing. Form: Ground plant.

ST. JOHN'S WORT. As a result of recent media attention, a widely used herb clinically proven to combat depression. Mood elevator and antidote for anxiety and nervous tension. Form: Dried leaves.

UVA URSI. Plant used since the Middle Ages as a diuretic. Disinfects the kidney and bladder. Form: Dried leaves.

VERVAIN. Verbena officinalis is enormously popular in Europe as an after-dinner digestive tisane. Also relieves depression and nervous exhaustion as well as migraines and stress-caused headaches. Form: Fresh or dried leaves.

WHITE WILLOW. Salicin, in the bark of the deciduous willow tree, is an analgesic and the original source of the synthetic chemicals in the aspirin we know today. Reduces fever and pain as well as upset stomach and heartburn. Form: Dried bark.

WILD CHERRY. Bark of the tall wild cherry tree is an old Native American remedy, still used by contemporary herbalists. Suppresses chronic coughs by calming the nerves that control the cough reflex. Form: Dried bark.

WINTERGREEN. Hardy evergreen shrub with fragrant leaves. Thought to be a painkiller and good source of potassium and magnesium. Form: Dried leaves.

YARROW. Delicate appearance of this lovely garden perennial belies its powerful healing properties. Induces sweating to cool a fever, lowers blood pressure, relieves stomach disorders, and heals surface wounds. Form: Dried leaves.

ZATAR. Species of thyme commonly used in North Africa and the Middle East for its powerful effects on stomach disorders. Eases stomach cramps and diarrhea. Form: Dried leaves.

Resource Guide

Asia Natural Products, Inc.
1603 Indiana Street
San Francisco, CA 94124
(415) 920-2638
Excellent quality, chemical-free Chinese herbs. Herb and price list available.

Ed Bauman
Institute for Educational Therapy
7981 Old Redwood Highway
Cotati, CA 94931
(707) 795-1284
Nutritional consultant training program.

Blessed Herbs
100 Baree Plains Road
Okham, MA 01068
(800) 489-HERB
Organic and wild-crafted herbs by the pound. Catalog.

California School of Herbal Studies
9309 Highway 116
Forestville, CA 95436
(707) 887-2012
Comprehensive and short-term courses.

Diana Deluca
P.O. Box 2
Sebastopol, CA 95473
Information on botanica erotica and kitchen medicinals.

Margaret Dexter
P.O. Box 846
Planetarium Station
New York, NY 10024-0540
(212) 496-6726
Margaret's Magicals, classes, and informative mailings.

East West Herb Course
Box 712
Santa Cruz, CA 95061
(800) 717-5010
Home study on herbal medicine and herbalism.

Elixir Farm Botanicals
Brixey, MO 65618
(417) 261-2393
Organic Chinese and indigenous medicinal plant seeds, roots, and plants. Catalog.

Herb Pharm
P.O. Box 116
Williams, OR 97544
(541) 846-3232
Chinese and culinary herbs, herbal extracts, and educational material. Catalog.

Herb Research Foundation
1007 Pearl Street, Suite 200
Boulder, CO 80302
(800) 748-2617
Educational resource on all aspects of herbs and herbalism.

Lotus Press
P.O. Box 325
Twin Lakes, WI 53181
(800) 548-3824
To purchase Amadea Morningstar's books on Ayurvedic cooking and herbal care.

Moonrise Herbs
826 G Street
Arcata, CA 95521
(800) 603-8364
Mail-order herbs and newsletter. Herb list.

Nam Singh
San Francisco, CA
(415) 661-7160
Classes and information on Chinese Herbal Cooking.

Pacific Botanicals
4350 Fish Hatchery Road
Grants Pass, OR 97527
(541) 479-7777
Certified organically grown and wild-crafted herbs. Catalog.

Queen of Sheba
1100 Sutter Street
San Francisco, CA 94109
(415) 56SHEBA
Zatar and other Middle Eastern herbs by mail.

San Francisco Herb Co.
250 14th Street
San Francisco, CA 94103
(800) 227-4530
Herbs, spices, and teas. Catalog.

Sultan's Delight
P.O. Box 090302
Brooklyn, NY 11209
(800) 852-5046
Middle Eastern herbs, spices, and ingredients by mail. Catalog.

Wishgarden Herbs
Catherine Hunziker, Herbalist
4699 Nautilus Court, Suite 202
Boulder, CO 80301
(303) 516-1803
Herbs and herbal blends. Catalog.

Further Reading

Arvigo, Rosa, and Michael Balick. *Rainforest Remedies.* Twin Lakes, Wisc.: Lotus Press, 1993.

Barnard, Neal, M.D. *Eat Right Live Longer.* New York: Harmony Books, 1995.

Beinfield, Harriet, and Efrem Korngold. *Between Heaven and Earth.* New York: Ballantine Books, 1991.

Bellamy, David, and Andrea Pfister. *World Medicine.* Blackwell Publishers, 1992.

Birdwood, G. T. *Practical Bazaar Medicines.* New Delhi: Asian Educational Services, 1987.

Bremmess, Lesley. *The Complete Book of Herbs.* New York: Viking Studio Books, 1988.

Charmine, Susan E. *Raw Juice Therapy.* New York: Baronet Publishing,1977.

Chopra, Deepak, M.D. *Perfect Health.* New York: Harmony Books, 1991.

Coon, Nelson. *Using Plants for Healing.* Hearthside Press, 1963.

Culpepper's Color Herbal. New York: Sterling Publishing, 1983.

Dawson, Warren R. *A Leechbook or Collection of Medical Recipes of the Fifteenth Century.* London: Macmillan, 1934.

Griggs, Barbara. *Green Pharmacy.* Rochester, Vt.: Healing Arts Press, 1981, 1991.

Haas, Elson M., M.D. *Staying Healthy with Nutrition.* Berkeley, Calif.: Celestial Arts, 1992.

Hand, Wayland D. *American Folk Medicine.* Los Angeles: University of California Press, 1976.

Handbook of Domestic Medicine and Common Ayurvedic Recipes. New Delhi: Central Council for Research in Indian Medicine and Homeopathy, 1978.

Hedley, Christopher, and Non Shaw. *Herbal Remedies.* Bristol, England: Paragon, 1996.

Jensen, Dr. Bernard. *Foods That Heal.* Garden City Park, N.Y.: Avery Publishing, 1988.

Lust, John. *The Herb Book.* New York: Bantam, 1974.

Mabey, Richard. *The New Age Herbalist.* London: Gaia Books Ltd., 1988.

Morningstar, Amadea. *Ayurvedic Cooking for Westerners.* Twin Lakes, Wisc.:, Lotus Press, 1995.

Ody, Penelope. *The Complete Medicinal Herbal.* London: Dorling Kindersley, 1993.

Page, Linda Rector. *Healthy Healing.* Healthy Healing Publications, 1985.

Patnaik, Naveen. *The Garden of Life.* New York: Doubleday, 1993.

Phillips, Roger, and Nicky Foy. *The Random House Book of Herbs.* New York: Random House, 1996.

Pierre, Michel. *Au Bonheur des plantes.* Paris: Editions Belfond, 1992.

Reid, Daniel P. *Chinese Herbal Medicine.* Boston: Shambala, 1993.

Republic of Tea. *The Book of Tea and Herbs.* Santa Rosa, Calif.: The Cole Group, 1993.

Rosner, Fred. *Medicine in the Bible and the Talmud.* New York: Yeshiva University Press, 1977.

Sanecki, Kay. *History of the English Herb Garden.* London: Ward Lock, 1992.

Vogel, Virgil J. *American Indian Medicine.* Norman, Okla.: University of Oklahoma Press, 1970.

Tolley, Emelie, and Chris Mead. *Herbs.* New York: Clarkson N. Potter, 1985.

Westrich, LoLo. *California Herbal Remedies.* Houston: Gulf Publishing, 1989.

Index